Richard J. Bord and Joseph E. Faulkner are in the department of sociology at The Pennsylvania State University. Dr. Bord teaches courses in social movements, social psychology, and complex organizations. Dr. Faulkner teaches sociology of religion, social theory, and urban sociology. Dr. Bord earned his Ph.D. at the University of Iowa, Dr. Faulkner at Penn State.

D1590435

THE CATHOLIC CHARISMATICS

THE
CATHOLIC CHARISMATICS
The Anatomy of a Modern Religious Movement

Richard J. Bord
and
Joseph E. Faulkner

The Pennsylvania State University Press
University Park and London

Library of Congress Cataloging in Publication Data

Bord, Richard J., 1937–
The Catholic Charismatics.

Includes bibliography and index.
1. Pentecostalism—Catholic Church. 2. Catholic
Church—Doctrinal and controversial works.
I. Faulkner, Joseph E. II. Title.
BX2350.57.B67 1983   282   82-42782
ISBN 0-271-00340-5

Designed by Dolly Carr

Printed in the United States of America

To all those CCR members who shared their lives
with us and made this book possible.

Contents

Preface
The Catholic Charismatic Renewal

Events that capture our attention most dramatically are often those that provide contrasts and oppositions: balances of light and dark in great art works, images of good and evil in philosophy and religion, the glaring neon sign against the night sky, the ordinarily calm individual who unexpectedly flies into a fit of rage. The immediate stimulus for our research was exactly this sort of dramatic contrast. The decade of the 1960s in the United States shall be etched forever in the pages of history as the turbulent 60s. Upper middle and middle class university students challenged the very institutions that made their way of life possible. Those of us who spent at least some of these years in university settings will not forget the daily round of speeches, the demonstrations in the streets, the boycotted classes, and the helmeted police patrolling our campuses.

However, in the midst of this political maelstrom emerged small groups of students who were seemingly oblivious to the burning issues of the day. In fact their happy, serene demeanor appeared completely incongruous in the context of the struggle for civil rights and for withdrawal of United States forces from Vietnam that dominated campus life. In discussions with them we were amazed to learn that they had been "baptized in the Holy Spirit," and many reported that they spoke in tongues, prophesied, and participated in faith healing. This was our initial introduction to the recent resurgence of groups interested in returning to a form of biblical Christianity. These groups have attracted thousands of faithful supporters, and in some ways may be a more potent challenge to existing authority than the more highly publicized social movements of the 1960s. One of the leaders in this thrust toward Biblical Christianity was the Catholic Charismatic Renewal, which "officially" began in 1967.

Like the other social movements of the 60s, the Catholic Charismatic Renewal drew its initial support from middle and upper middle class college students. Its birth was primarily a university phenomenon, and for a time it spread primarily in universities. Unlike their more vocal student contemporaries who stressed social change through collective activism, these religious enthusiasts stressed social change through the transformation of individuals. The spectacle of educated, middle-class students speaking in tongues, prophesying, and practicing faith healing stimulated our professional interest. For had we not been taught that only poorly educated, down and out, usually Southern born individuals engaged in this kind of behavior? The Catholic Charismatic Renewal seemed an excellent research opportunity that could have significant dividends for theories of religion, social movement development, and social change. We therefore began a study that culminated in this book.

Our study consisted of a three-year formal investigation, preceded and followed by periods of informal research totaling more than a dozen years. Between 1967 and 1971 we attended meetings and conferences of Catholic Charismatic Renewal, talked with leaders and other members, and read movement literature—intensively albeit somewhat unsystematically—and since 1974 we have done the same. From 1972 through 1974, supported by a grant from the Institute for the Arts and Humanistic Studies and by funds from the Central Fund for Research and the sociology department at Penn State University, we designed and executed a key informant, participant observation, and questionnaire study of the Catholic Charismatic Renewal (this is the term preferred by most participants), or the CCR as it shall be designated in the remainder of this book.

To obtain questionnaire data we used the *Directory of Catholic Charismatic Prayer Groups* (1972) as a guide and selected 15 prayer groups located in various parts of Indiana, Louisiana, Maryland, Michigan, New Jersey, New York, Pennsylvania, and Wisconsin (cost constraints limited geographical spread). The primary selection criterion was group size: large (200–plus), medium (100–199), and small (less than 100). There were five groups in each size range. Following selection, we visited 11 of these groups and distributed (with the consent of the leadership) a questionnaire to those present who were willing to fill it out. In the remaining four groups we left questionnaires with group leaders, who later distributed them to willing members. We eventually received 987 completed questionnaires. This is somewhat over 50 percent of those we are sure were distributed.

In addition to the questionnaire data, each of us attended over 20 separate prayer meetings in different parts of the country, plus two international conventions. Twelve of the meetings were taped in their entirety, with the consent of the leadership. We always attempted to engage in extended discussion with both leaders and members. At one point we spent a weekend in an established Charismatic community in the Midwest. Because a number of Bord's friends have been deeply involved in the movement almost from its inception, we could use the key informant technique at various points in the research. For example, two of those friends were closely involved in the inception and decline of the Notre Dame Community (True House) and provided valuable information about events there.

As we traveled from group to group, we were continually struck by the openness and genuine warmth of the people we met. We both have fond memories of discussions with leaders lasting until three and four in the morning, shared teabags and leftover stew at a household dinner in a Charismatic community, the steady stream of prayers that were offered for the success of our research and our safe travel, and the ever-present gentle attempts to help us "see the light." However, we both struggled to maintain our objectivity. On a number of occasions we were asked how it was possible to participate in so many meetings and not experience baptism in the spirit. The inquiry was usually followed by some low-key chiding about letting the intellect interfere with the work of the Holy Spirit, but no one ever made us feel uncomfortable or unwelcome. The entire research experience was a positive one.

Since we analyze the CCR from a sociological and social psychological perspective, the Holy Spirit will not be given credit as the prime mover of events described. Instead we will focus on social structural factors that help shape human motivation and behavior, plus certain aspects of human information processing that are essential if one is to understand how social structure operates within the individual. We realize that our many friends in the movement will view this type of analysis as misguided. However, we realize that we cannot explain all the variation in the phenomena we address, and so we do leave room for alternative explanations. Analysis from a scientific perspective does not, of course, invalidate other types of analysis based on different epistemological foundations.

There are several caveats for the reader attempting to evaluate the validity and representativeness of what we report in these pages. First, we do not have a random sample of either CCR participants or prayer groups. Cost considerations and problems of establishing population parameters made random sampling an impossibility. Second, even though we take great pains to establish the truth of events reported to us, and to accurately report events recorded or observed, the reader must be aware that we are selecting a subset of these things to report, and that some unintended bias may have entered in the selection process.

Third, we are painfully aware that even as we write these words the complex events which constitute this movement are in flux. Our attempt to freeze the movement in a time frame may omit important facts that are now somehow altering its shape and course. We have, however, attempted to keep abreast of important developments and to discuss some of the most recent in later pages.

This book is divided essentially into three parts. Chapters 1 and 2 describe the movement and our method of analysis; chapters 3, 4, 5, and 6 apply the analysis; and chapters 7 and 8 recapitulate and speculate on the future of the movement. Chapter 1 is a description and overview of the movement. We decided to include this material because little is apparently known about the CCR outside of rather restricted circles. The most common reaction, even among Roman Catholic laypeople, to a mention of Catholic pentecostalism is incredulity and the assumption that such a phenomenon must involve a tiny minority of overcommitted zealots. Chapter 2 is a detailed discussion of the theoretical underpinnings guiding our analysis of the CCR. It provides the reader with a systematic statement of our perspective and sets the stage for the remaining analysis.

The remaining chapters flesh out the skeleton comprising the model of social movement evolution. Chapter 3 discusses the various strains that led people sharing overlapping communication networks to define their world as unmanageable. Chapter 4 details the events that increased their perception that alternatives were available and describes the forms their search behavior took. Chapter 5 presents an analysis of the commitment activities and the formation of leadership around these activities. Chapter 6 describes impression management activities, including the relationship between the growing movement and existing authority. Chapter 7 discusses the CCR's relation to the Catholic Church and its organizational forms. Finally, chapter 8 attempts to go beyond the findings of our research and prognosticate about the future of the movement.

This entire project was undertaken with the hope of making a useful addition to an understanding of social movements in general, religious movements in particular, and the interplay of the sacred and secular in one of the most scientific-technological societies ever developed. You, the reader, will ultimately decide whether that goal has been achieved.

1
Neopentecostalism and the CCR

The setting is a brightly lit cafeteria in a Roman Catholic grade school situated on the outskirts of a large urban-industrial complex in the North Central United States. Approximately 200 people varying in age from 9 to 67 (but heavily clustered in the 25 to 35 age categories), of both sexes (but approximately 60 percent women), all white, well dressed, and generally conventionally groomed, gather in the spacious room. Most people are sitting in chairs radiating in a series of concentric circles. The room is filled with an abundance of laughter, handshaking, hugging, and greetings shouted across the room as people enter and seek out chairs. The phrase "praise the Lord" punctuates coversation throughout the room. As a visitor you are warmly welcomed and introduced to whoever is within easy reach.

Soon everyone is seated, and several people in the innermost circle of chairs pick up guitars, banjos, or tambourines. A guitarist strokes a few chords, the crowd becomes quiet, and the instrumentalists begin singing "Alleluia, Alleluia, give thanks to the living Lord." The crowd enthusiastically joins in. After the hymn everyone prays aloud, but not in unison. The phrases most often distinguished are "praise you, Lord," "praise you, Jesus," "thank you, Lord," and "Alleluia." Although the praying is enthusiastic, it is not hysterical. Everyone speaks slightly above ordinary conversational amplitude. After the prayers die out, a tall, heavyset man announces: "I am glad tonight that I know the one that song is being sung about. We are here tonight to be with him. . . . Saturday nights he has a chance to come and be with us in a body. He has an opportunity to be glorified in our midst."

After another song of praise the group again launches into independent but simultaneous prayer. Soon the distinguishable phrases are replaced with utterances that appear to follow conventional grammatical forms but employ an unconventional vocabulary. When approximately 60 to 70 percent of the group is "speaking in tongues," part of the group begins monotonically singing in tongues at roughly middle C on a piano keyboard. Quickly two or three other subgroups establish other tonal positions in their tongue speaking so that a rough harmony is formed. Once the harmonic chord is formed, some individual tongue singers, primarily those with soprano voices, form variations around the basic chord. The sound builds in intensity and then fades, tongue singing becomes tongue speaking once again, and tongue speaking becomes familiar phrases of "thank you, Lord," "praise you, Jesus," and then trails off into silence.

The tall, heavyset man asks everyone to turn to Peter's First Epistle, Second Chapter, and begins reading Scripture to the group. He ends the reading with:

> You, however, are a chosen race . . . a royal priesthood . . . a holy nation . . . a people he claims for his own. Once you were no people but now you are God's people. You were nobodies but he made you somebodies. He calls each of us to be a people.

This message is greeted with an especially enthusiastic round of "praise you, Lord" and other statements of praise.

After several other Scripture readings and prayers of praise, a Roman Catholic monk situated in the center circle loudly and clearly proclaims:

> Shunta kurapa keera ah shuntata
> Haley, haley pakeera ho shunta kurapa keera, oh shuntatara
> Haley, Haley halinameera, hola hokatakeera palasheery
> Haley pakeera panamadamada, holapadueera,
>   hola pacheera panakeery, hachinta pokatakeera.

The monk's tongue speaking is followed by three successive interpretations. They follow in their order of occurrence:

> My children, I love you, and I want you near me.
> At my side is what you're made for,
> to be near me, everyday, to be near me.
> Don't be afraid, I can handle everything.

> My children, know that I will act in your midst.
> Know that I will act in your midst because I am the Lord.
> I will act for my sake, not for yours. For mine
> that I might be lifted up, that I might be glorified,
> that I might be praised and adored.
> Know that my children, I am the Lord and I will act.

My children, I would have you know I stand in your midst.
I would have you know that it is more than just a song I touch
you with. That even now my hand is stretched to touch you my
children. I want you to know this, that if you will lift your
hand up to me I will touch you and your life will never be the
same again. And when I come into your life I will make a
profound difference to you. Know that I am in your midst that
I might touch you my children. Let me touch you.

The group leader then asks the crowd to "let the Lord touch us. Let's throw aside the cloak that shields us from one another and open our hearts and let Jesus touch us."

There is more prayer and praise, followed by a series of testimonies concerning how the Lord has worked in the lives of the participants during the preceding week. One group leader narrates how the Lord had told him what to say while he was taking a nap, and that the experience had left him feeling "warm all over." One woman in the crowd confirms that the Holy Spirit is making the whole evening a success in spite of everyone's fatigue. Another woman tells of being healed of foot and abdominal pains. Another had felt guilty and unworthy, but the Lord forgave her and now she feels ecstatic. A man had his "nasty temperament" cured, and money is no longer the driving force in his life. One man who taught a religion class to Roman Catholic children attending public school tells the following story:

> Around Halloween time I started teaching them how to recognize the
> kingdom of darkness. They had been involved with ouija boards, horo-
> scopes, fortune telling, and things like that. So I told them how I had been
> involved with things like that before I met Jesus Christ and how it tried to
> kill me and tear apart my life. I told them of how the mighty name of
> Jesus Christ could drive them away.

After narrating the process through which he had convinced a teacher to renounce the occult, he ends his testimony with: "I'm not teaching them that Jesus is ecology, or humanism, or anything counterfeit." Finally, a young woman affirmed that Jesus really wanted to establish a personal relationship with them, even to the point of feeling comfortable when calling him "Daddy."

More songs, prayer and praise, and tongue speaking is followed by the leader telling the group about a nun who is having a tremendous personal crisis and who needs prayer. He beckons toward two nuns who are seated to his right, about halfway back in the room. The smaller of the two nuns gets up and hesitantly approaches the inner circle. She stares at the floor as tears slowly streak her face. The members of the inner circle

gather around the dejected figure, place their hands on her head and
shoulders, and pray for her healing. Eventually the entire group is praying for the nun. Afterward, the nun tearfully stumbles to her seat. More
songs are sung, and the group begins to break up and head for the door.
Everyone is happy but somewhat subdued with fatigue, chairs are
stacked, and the room again becomes a well-scrubbed school cafeteria.

The scene described above is repeated, with minor modifications, daily
in cities and towns throughout the United States, Canada, and a growing
list of foreign countries. Devout Roman Catholics, most of them middle
class in their level of occupation, education, and income, meet in private
homes, school buildings, and in both Protestant and Catholic churches to
engage in public prayer, Bible reading, speaking in tongues, prophesying,
and healings of various sorts. In the last ten years pentecostalism has
become a major issue in the Roman Catholic Church and has stimulated
a number of volumes attempting to describe it, to guide it, to praise or
to challenge it. (For example, Ranaghan and Ranaghan, 1969; O'Connor,
1971; Ford, 1970; Fichter, 1975). Pentecostalism in general, the so-called
third force in Christianity, has flourished at a time when the more
traditional expressions of Christianity have been suffering "alarming declines" (Sheerin, 1970). A brief historical overview will aid the uniniti-
ated reader in locating Roman Catholic pentecostalism in the broader
spectrum of pentecostalism as a movement in Christianity.

The Historical Roots of Pentecostalism

> There is, I would say, a recurrent situation in Church history—using the
> word "church" in the widest sense—where an excess of charity threatens
> unity. You have a clique, an elite, of Christian men and (more impor-
> tantly) women who are trying to live a less worldly life than their neigh-
> bors; to be more attentive to the guidance (directly felt, they would tell
> you) of the Holy Spirit (Knox, 1950:1).

The history of Christianity is punctuated by what Knox (1950) calls
"enthusiastic" movements. The existing institutional church is defined as
having capitulated to secular society, as having lost the supernatural
vision in the demands of mundane activity. An ideal of the earliest
church is held up as the behavioral model that all good Christians should
emulate. Emphasis is on the individual's direct contact with—and guidance from—the divine, on heart and feeling over head and reason, and
on the imminent Second Coming of Christ (Knox, 1950). Institutional
authority and doctrinal complexities are devalued in an emotional thrust
toward democratic Christianity.

Although the enthusiasm syndrome has a long, dramatic history, it took on a more enduring and more encompassing social form after the Protestant Reformation. The Quakers, Shakers, and even the Mormons experienced the "enthusiasm of the Spirit." Brigham Young reportedly spoke in tongues and interpreted his own message to his congregation (Synan, 1971:25). But it was the Methodism of Wesley and Whitefield in the eighteenth century that ignited a flame which eventually flared into pentecostalism. Out of the numerous postbellum revivals came dissident Methodists who felt that Wesley's doctrine of sanctification or perfection had been deemphasized. The central idea of these "holiness" groups was that complete holiness was possible only after the individual forfeits self and allows the Holy Spirit to live within and direct life in the pattern dictated by Christ's example. Receipt of the Holy Spirit—that is baptism in the spirit—was believed to be evident by a clearly recognizable emotional reaciton (Nichol, 1966).

Shortly after its inception divisiveness struck the Holiness movement in the form of controversy concerning what was required to prove that one had been baptized in the Holy Spirit. Tongue speaking, already a characteristic of camp meetings, was held by many to be *the* evidence of one's reception of the spirit. This belief received much support in the Bible School in Topeka, Kansas, under the leadership of its founder, Charles Parham. One of Parham's students, W.J. Seymour, was invited to Los Angeles to speak in a Holiness church. His reception was cool, since he insisted that anyone who could not speak in tongues was not spirit baptized (even though Seymour himself apparently had not received the gift at that time). No longer welcomed by the group who had invited him, Seymour proceeded to organize his own revival in an old Methodist Church on Azusa Street in Los Angeles. What transpired there attracted national attention. Meetings were held at the Azusa Street Mission for three years and attracted thousands of participants, some from as far away as Europe. These meetings were characterized by intense emotionalism; tongue speaking, healings, and various miracles occurred nightly. It is generally agreed that the pentecostal movement began at the Azusa Street Mission.

The subsequent development of pentecostalism in America is well documented elsewhere (see Nichol, 1966; Synan, 1971; Hollenweger, 1972). Of particular importance to us is that pentecostals, at first shunned and ridiculed by their more institutionally oriented brethren, grew steadily to ever-increasing respectability in American religious circles. In recent years the established mainline Protestant bodies began giving attention to Spirit Baptism and tongue speaking. It is these groups to whom the term "neopentecostalism" has been attached. The Episcopal Church, presumably the least likely candidate among the Protestant denominations, reports pentecostal activities among its members, and devotes increasing attention to this topic in the pages of the *Episcopalian*. The Full Gospel Business Men's Fellowship International, a lay organization of prominent businessmen, has done much to publicize the fact that pentecostal practitioners are very much a part of the mainstream of society. The FGBMFI helped to finance the Oral Roberts University in Tulsa, Oklahoma, and supports Roberts's works in the healing ministry. Oral Roberts himself, beginning as a nondenominational pentecostal minister, has recently been accepted into the United Methodist Church with full ministerial credentials.

Yet it would be a mistake for the reader to assume at this point that pentecostalism is a homogeneous phenomenon. Although pentecostals generally agree on the importance of baptism in the holy spirit (and the various "gifts of the spirit"), agree on the importance of Scripture as revelation of God's word, and manifest a literal belief in evil spirits, there are important differences between the many pentecostal subgroups. Forms of worship vary all the way from the violent emotionalism characterizing the pentecostal snake handler, found primarily among poor whites in parts of the South, to the relatively low-key expressions exhibited by middle class pentecostals allied with the main line denominations. Furthermore, the doctrinal differences separating various Protestant denominations, and Protestants and Catholics, also separate the pentecostal faithful from these denominations although these doctrinal differences are generally not emphasized.

Differences also exist over acceptable life styles. A stress on asceticism is much more common among working and lower class pentecostals. Asceticism has been adopted by some neopentecostal individuals, but it is generally underemphasized in favor of simplcity in life style. A glimpse of the elegantly dressed participants displayed in the televised National Convention of the Full Gospel Business Men's Fellowship International (December 1975) would have quickly dispelled the notion that pentecostals thrive on deprivation and suffering. Pentecostals also vary in their view of the future. Immanent apocalyptic visions are more common almong lower and working class pentecostals (Elinson, 1965), while the more middle class neopentecostals place greater emphasis on a joyful future when all Christians will be united under the pentecostal umbrella. As one Roman Catholic priest put it at the close of a pentecostal prayer meeting:

> I've noticed of late, and perhaps you have too, in the charismatic renewal, the movement of God within Chirstianity itself, there is a great deal of emphasis being placed on the Book of Revelation and I know many Christians, particularly in Pittsburgh and other places that I've been, wondering who the beast really is and do I die before the tribulation, and how

long is that tribulation going to be. What I like about you people is that you don't even fool around with those things, you go straight to Revelation 21, and you say that the kingdom is coming down, a new heaven and a new earth will be established, and that is the kind of emphasis I like. I like, for myself, an emphasis on the new heaven and the earth and I don't care who the beast is.

Roman Catholicism has been one of the last major denominations to be "invaded" by pentecostalism. Some authors have referred to Catholic pentecostalism as the third great wave in pentecostal history, the first two waves being classical and neopentecostal activity in Protestant circles. Contrary to both popular belief and academic expectations, pentecostalism was embraced by Roman Catholics with a vigor surpassing that of most main line Protestant denominations. It is impossible to accurately assess the number of Roman Catholics who identify themselves as pentecostals. One movement spokesperson estimated that there were 200,000 members in North America in 1972 (Ranaghan, 1972), while the *New York Times* later (1974) placed worldwide membership near 350,000. Using as a guide the movement's own record, the *Directory of Catholic Charismatic Prayer Groups*, we see that the 1977 United States Roman Catholic membership alone totals 110,402.[1] CCR spokespersons would argue that this is a conservative estimate, since a small minority of groups listed in the *Directory* do not report numbers of members, and groups certainly exist which are not listed in that document. We suspect, however, that by 1977 the CCR had received enough attention so that existing groups would be aware of the *Directory* and eager to be entered in it. Again using the *Directory* as an information source, we constructed figure 1, which illustrates the growth in number of prayer groups from 1970 to 1977 in the United States only. We are unable to graphically present the growth in number of members for that time period because the *Directory* first began accumulating this type of information in 1973. However, for the years 1973 through 1977 we include the number of Roman Catholic members in the United States only. Although the size range of prayer groups varies tremendously (from 3 to over 1500), the hypothetical average group has approximately 50 members.

The growth curve in figure 1 clearly indicates that the years between 1972 and 1974 were the bumper crop years for the CCR. Between 1973

[1]This is an annual publication, with the exception of the years 1975 and 1976, which were combined into a single issue. It was initially published by the Communication Center at Notre Dame, Indiana, but is now published by the National Communications Office in South Bend, Indiana. Groups self-report their name, meeting place, leaders' names and telephone numbers, the percentage of the group that is Roman Catholic and the number of members.

Figure 1 Growth in Number of Prayer Groups in the United States between 1970 and 1977.

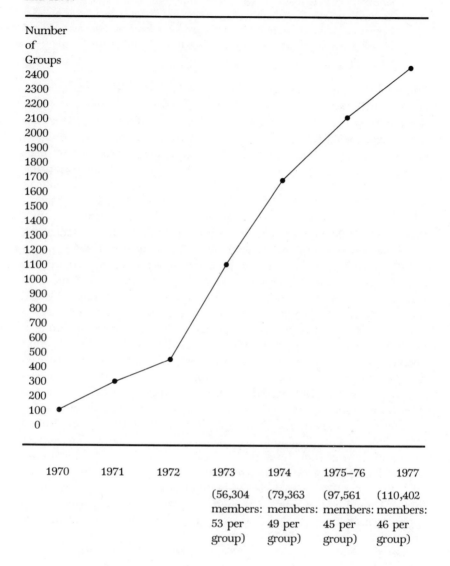

			1973	1974	1975–76	1977
1970	1971	1972	(56,304 members: 53 per group)	(79,363 members: 49 per group)	(97,561 members: 45 per group)	(110,402 members: 46 per group)

Table 1 Percentage Breakdown of Selected Demographic Characteristics of CCR
Members.

Sex		Age		Level of education		Father's Education
Females	62%	Less than 15	2%	Grade school only	0.8%	22.1%
Males	38%	15–18	5.6%	Finished jr. high	1.4%	7.7%
		19–21	18.8%	Some high school	4.9%	10.2%
		22–25	21.1%	High school grad.	15.8%	20.5%
		26–30	11.8%	Some college	37.0%	12.9%
		31–35	8.9%	College grad.	24.9%	14.1%
		36–40	6.6%	Advanced degree	14.3%	12.5%
		41–50	14.7%			
		51–60	8.6%			
		61+	3.7%			

and 1974, 23,059 members (again, United States only) were added to the
existing pool; between 1974 and 1975–1976 (note the combined years),
18,198 additional members were added over the previous year's total;
and between 1975–1976 and 1977, only 12,841 additional members
graced the pages of the *Directory*. The decline in rate of growth after
1974 has some implications which will be discussed in chapter 6.

Member Characteristics

The characteristics of movement participants exhibited by our questionnaire data generally parallel what other observers have noted. Table 1
presents percentage breakdowns for the sample on age, sex, and level of
education for participants.

As is true of most religious activity in industrialized societies, females
make up a generous majority of CCR members. We have good reason to
believe that these figures accurately represent the sex ratio of the movement across the United States, since a similar 60–40 ratio was also
observed at two international conventions and in most prayer meetings
we attended. The disproportionate number of women participants has
caused a chronic problem for CCR leadership, especially in cases where
the wife is a member but the husband is not.

The level of education for both participants and their fathers is quite
high. However, our own observations and the reported observations of
other students of the CCR (Harrison, 1974) lead us to believe that this
percentage breakdown is a reasonably accurate reflection of the level of

education of CCR members. The fact that a personalized, relatively emotional religious form appeals primarily to those having at least some college education raises some interesting speculations about the American middle class and social change in contemporary America.

The age distribution was bimodal, with a majority of respondents under thirty years of age. The bimodal nature of our sample supports issues dealing with certain kinds of social-personal strain and their relationship to movement development. All of the issues mentioned above will be discussed in detail in chapter 3.

The Beginning

The adoption of pentecostal techniques by Roman Catholics originated under the direct influence of Protestant pentecostals and subsequently spread through clearly defined, preexisting sociometric networks (Ranaghan and Ranaghan, 1969; O'Connor, 1971). A small number of lay faculty at Duquesne University in 1967 had been earnestly and intensely praying for a return to the type of Christian community and vitality akin to that described in the Bible as characteristic of the first Christians. During this same period they were introduced to two books that are still found on the recommended reading lists for Catholic Charismatics: *The Cross and the Switchblade* (Wilkerson, 1964) and *They Speak in Other Tongues* (Sherrill, 1965).

The former book, to be discussed in chapter 4, describes an Evangelical Protestant minister's adventures as he worked with gang youth in New York City. A number of "miracles" are described in the book and are attributed to the work of the Holy Spirit. The latter book is a chronicle of one man's experience in finding Christ in a more intense way through pentecostalism. Its theme is that God is not to be found through logic or exercise of the intellect but through a "leap of faith," a renunciation of self in favor of something greater. It, too, describes a number of "miracles" and devotes considerable attention to speaking in tongues.

With a strengthened conviction in the ability of renewed Christianity to solve modern day problems, and with a working knowledge of pentecostal orientation and techniques, these lay faculty members sought out Protestant pentecostals, and two of them were subsequently baptized in the Holy Spirit. These two "laid hands" on two others who were baptized in the Holy Spirit. ("Laying on of hands" consists of the suppliant either standing, sitting, or kneeling while others place their hands on his or her head and shoulders and intensely pray for the suppliant's conversion, healing, reception of the Holy Spirit, or some other solution to a problem the individual may have. The basic idea is that the Holy Spirit "flows" from the faithful to the suppliant.) Shortly afterward, these four faculty members met with approximately 30 students on a religious retreat at Duquesne University. These students had also read *The Cross and the Switchblade* and were there to seek the will of Jesus Christ in their lives. This group experienced baptism in the spirit in what was to eventually become known as the Duquesne Weekend, the official beginning of the Catholic Charismatic Renewal.

From this nucleus of individuals the movement spread initially throughout college campuses in the Midwest: Notre Dame, Michigan State, and Iowa State, in particular. From these institutions it diffused to other parts of the United States, always following previously existing social networks. Ample research demonstrates that cultural and social organizational innovations diffuse much more efficiently through existing interpersonal networks than by any other means. Apparently this method of recruitment has been maintained as the movement grew between 1967 and 1973 (Harrison, 1974). Our own data demonstrates that 60.1 percent found their way into the movement via a relative or a friend, and 85.4 percent report that one or more of their best friends are in the movement. Ten percent were introduced to the movement through participation in other religious gatherings such as weekend retreats. Seven percent characterized themselves as religious seekers who heard about the movement and then went to a prayer meeting. Less than 4 percent were initially involved through a clergyman. The remainder of the sample gave very idiosyncratic or uncodable responses.

Actually, the term Catholic Charismatic Renewal is something of a misnomer and may be misleading. Protestants have been involved in this movement from the very beginning and continue to be coparticipators in many prayer groups and communities. For example, a full 13 percent of our sample claim Protestant Church affiliation. This percentage is approximately the same as the percentage of Protestants reported in *The Directory of Catholic Prayer Groups* who are regular members of predominantly Roman Catholic groups. When broken down into denominational affiliation, these 127 Protestants are distributed principally over the four major denominations comprising the bulk of neopentecostalism. Twenty-five percent are Lutheran, 25 percent are Methodist, 19 percent are Presbyterian, 17 percent are Episcopalian, while the remaining 14 percent report a wide variety of allegiances.

Influential Protestant pentecostals, some of them classical pentecostals, also exert considerable influence in the CCR through speeches given at CCR regional and national meetings and through articles contributed to *New Covenant* magazine. People like David duPlessis and Derek Prince, world renowned pentecostal leaders, are familiar names to those involved in the CCR.

Interdenominational participation is strongly encouraged by the principal lay leaders of the CCR. Ecumenicism must certainly be considered one of the major thrusts of this movement. Christian unity is viewed as a requirement for Christian survival in modern, secular society. The declining impact of Christian values, beliefs, and practices is considered a direct result of the fragmentation that has characterized Christianity, especially since the Protestant Reformation in the sixteenth century. The CCR is viewed as one vehicle that can eventually bring committed Christians together again.

A Cult, a Sect, or What?

The ideological focus of the CCR is renewal. Although "renewal" encompasses a number of different dimensions (see Clark, in Ranaghan and Ranaghan, 1971), the term refers to an overall spiritual regeneration of a dying institutional church—a church suffering a "crisis of faith." Church leadership in general is viewed as having capitulated to secularism and as having lost the vision and reality of the resurrected Christ.

Renewal, by definition, negates separation. CCR leaders have taken great pains to establish ongoing, amicable relationships with the church hierarchy. These struggles for recognition and acceptance were often met by cool indifference or outright hostility, especially from parish priests. However, the CCR has had support from those in high places since the genesis of the movement. Cardinal Leon Joseph Suenens of Belgium, a liberal prelate intensely concerned with implementing the mandates of Vatican II, has been a vocal supporter. He addressed the 1973 National Convention and also visited influential Charismatic communities in the United States. The intense desire of most CCR participants to be accepted by the hierarchy is exemplified by the tumultuous standing ovation given Cardinal Suenens at the 1973 convention and by the excitement generated by the visit of Ralph Martin, one of the CCR leaders, to the Pope that same year. After a considerable period of cautiousness the church finally established an official liaison with the movement in 1975.

The renewal theme is continually reiterated by the literature emanating from the movement. The message is clear: CCR leaders do not want the movement identified with any sectarian, separatist emphasis. Movement leaders are quick to point out that membership in the CCR often results in even greater church allegiance than existed prior to such membership, and Fichter (1975:28–30) documents the authenticity of these claims.

Our data also supports the prochurch effect of membership in the CCR, but in addition it provides some interesting contradictions. For example, 85.9 percent of our sample state that church membership is extremely or quite important. Only 4.1 percent claim it to be unimportant. Most are regular churchgoers; 93.3 percent attend church three or more times monthly, while 25.6 percent are daily participants. Fifty-five percent claim to attend church more since becoming pentecostal, and only 2.7 percent attend less. Sixty-four percent receive communion five or more times monthly; 55.8 percent recieve communion more since embracing pentecostalism, with 1.5 percent receiving less. Seventy-one percent regularly contribute to the church, and 58 percent belong to various types of parish organizations.

While the prochurch orientation of CCR members cannot be denied, it is equally clear that this allegiance is somewhat selective. Fichter (1975:29) reports that 55 percent of his sample agrees they would obey their bishop if he were to prohibit Charismatic prayer meetings, but only 22.7 percent of our sample agrees with the same statement (26.3 percent are somewhat undecided, and a full 47 percent disagree). Only 9.6 percent would obey the same command from their pastor, while a full 63.4 percent would disobey him. (An influential priest allied with the CCR suggests that if we were to distribute our questionnaire now, we would obtain a much smaller percentage indicating they would disobey their bishop or pastor.) The difference between Fichter's data and our own is probably the result of the difference in the two respective samples. Fichter sent questionnaires to movement leaders early in the developmental period of the CCR. At that time movement leaders were consciously fostering images of church loyalty so as not to bring official disfavor from the church hierarchy. Our sample taps a much wider segment of movement membership and therefore a wider spectrum of individual attitudes.

Another index of a prochurch orientation is the respondent's agreement or disagreement with church proclamations on matters of faith and morals. Of particular interest are their positions on issues that have generated a great deal of controversy within the church during the last decade and a half: contraception, abortion, and clerical celibacy. The official church positions on these three issues has been consistent and unwavering: rhythm is the only acceptable method of family regulation for married Catholics, abortion is wrong under any circumstance, and celibacy for priests is to continue.

It could be expected that a group committed to the church with the intensity indicated by the above figures would also enthusiastically embrace the official positions on these controversial issues. Table 2 demonstrates that such is not the case. Only 31.4 percent agree that rhythm is the only acceptable method of family regulation for married Catholics, while 13.9 percent agree that any method of birth control is acceptable for married Catholics. (The percentages for these questions include only the Roman Catholic respondents. N = 828.) Less than one-third of the sample disagrees with the statement that priests should be allowed to marry. The one issue that engenders the greatest correspondence be-

Table 2 Catholic Charismatics's Attitudes toward Selected Church Issues (in percentages).

Attitudes	% Agree	% Somewhat Undecided	% Disagree	Total
Rhythm is the only acceptable birth control method for married Catholics.	31.4	30.1	38.5	100 (N =828)
Any method of birth control is acceptable for married Catholics.	13.9	24.1	62.0	100 (N = 828)
Abortion is not acceptable under any circumstances.	72.2	17.8	10.0	100 (N = 828)
Priests should be allowed to marry.	30.5	37.6	31.9	100 (N = 828)

tween Catholic Charismatics and official church proclamation is that of abortion. A full 72 percent agree that abortion is not acceptable under any circumstances.

The picture emerging from the data so far is a mixed one. Catholic Charismatics strongly desire acceptance from the institutional church and are highly committed to the church in a devotional sense. There is, however, clear indication that allegiance to church authority is far from complete. We cannot completely agree with Fichter's somewhat unequivocal characterization of the CCR as a cult. Strong potentials for sectarianism exist in the CCR. It appears that many Catholic Charismatics's loyalty to the church is predicated on the church's somewhat uncritical acceptance of them and their practices. (The question of separatism as the result of interaction between the dissenting movement and the parent body will be discussed in Chapter 7.) The Catholic Church has done nothing at this point to reinforce dramatically any existing sect tendencies. This alone may account for the relatively unequivocal "churchiness" exhibited by Catholic Charismatics.

Leadership

Fichter (1975) has commented on the hesitancy of CCR members to discuss structure and patterns of influence within the movement. This hesitancy appears to result from the belief that the Lord directs every-thing. Leadership, therefore, is simply an enactment of the will of God and not a phenomena emerging from human structures of status, power, and control. If influence is a product of God's will, then there is little reason to subject it to critical analysis. It is clear, however, that strong and somewhat rigid patterns of influence characterize the social structure of the CCR.

Because of the grass roots nature of the CCR, leadership patterns are complex and somewhat diffuse. Gerlach and Hine (1970) provide a de-scriptively accurate analytical scheme by characterizing such movements as decentralized, segmented, and reticulate (weblike). The movement never had a single "great man" that can be identified as its founder and around whom all the faithful gather. Nor does it have a centralized structure in which the hierarchy monitors and controls activity at the level of individual prayer groups. Within the movement as a whole the hierarchical influence that does exist is not a result of sanctioning power but a product of information control. (French and Raven, 1959, provide an in-depth discussion of various types of power.)

Almost immediately after the Duquesne Weekend, a small group of laymen, who had previously been associated in a Christian community while students at Notre Dame in the mid 1960s, heard of the events at Duquesne and soon became baptized in the spirit. These men had a history of intense religious activity and commitment to church renewal. They were also involved (some in leadership positions) in the Cursillo movement (see chapter 4), a movement antedating the CCR which also stressed renewal via a "new Pentecost." It was this group of men that began the task of defining, shaping, and organizing the movement. This leadership core, until very recently, constituted the dominant influence on the National Service Committee, an executive steering committee con-sisting of seven self-perpetuating members and an advisory group of 37 members. This leadership core originated and continues to supply the movement's monthly newsletter, a sophisticated, attractive journal now produced in color with a computerized subscription list. They write much of and control all of the accepted reading and listening materials that are available for rent or purchase at prayer groups all over the country. They have developed a "Life in the Spirit" seminar booklet, which details strategies for involving and committing new members. They organize and orchestrate the annual international convention and act as guest speakers and advisors to local and regional prayer groups. The People of Praise community at South Bend, Indiana, and the Word of God community at Ann Arbor, Michigan, house this leadership core, with the Ann Arbor group having the greatest concentration and degree of influence.

Within the core, one person stands out as the movement theoretician and master designer, the principal organizer and former major authority of the Ann Arbor community, Steve Clark. Clark converted to Catholicism in 1960 and met with the others while doing graduate work in philosophy at Notre Dame. His organizational skills were already evident in his role as the head of the National Secretariat of the Cursillo movement in the mid 60s. Clark's numerous writings outline a dismal view of modern Christianity in general and Catholicism in particular. For example, "I felt the Church was probably in the first stages of a nervous breakdown. Nothing really worked. There were only piecemeal solutions instead of effective plans. The edifice was starting to crumble" (cited in Manney, *New Covenant*, February, 1973:14). According to Clark, if the church is to survive in any viable form, it must become evangelical and especially communitarian. Clark's vision is of Christians gathered in communal, mutually supporting islands of defense designed to minimize the impact of secular society and to serve as models to attract like-minded followers. This utopian goal underlies the motivation of those most committed to the Charismatic renewal and the goal that Clark and others are trying to realize in their community at Ann Arbor. Clark's own dedication has led him and some others to take a vow of celibacy.

The Ann Arbor community is the most influential of the "covenanted" communities in the United States. Estimate of the number of such communities existing in the United States varies. *The National Catholic Reporter* (September 5, 1975, p. 3) estimates the number between 20 and 40. It serves as both inspiration and ideal for similar communities and also for local prayer groups. Unlike past utopian communities (e.g., the Amanas, the Oneidas), CCR communitarians do not live in a single isolated geographic point and share meals as a body. Communities are comprised of households, a small group of people under a head living in an ordinary domicile somewhere in the city. Household composition varies: in a visit to the Ann Arbor community one author stayed in a household consisting of a married couple, with the husband as the head, and six single people of both sexes; while the other author was berthed in a household having entirely single men under an appointed head. Some members meet frequently for shared prayer and meals. Members live somewhat austere lives—that is, no television, plain functional clothing, closely regulated and few reading materials, and simple meals.

Authority within the community is highly structured and centralized, with submission being virtually complete. At the pinnacle of the Ann Arbor community, until 1976, was Steve Clark, one of three head coordinators. (The term "coordinator" is used, rather than "elder," which is more accurately descriptive of the role, to lessen the possibility of outsiders attributing intentions of being or becoming a separate church.)

Immediately under Clark are two head coordinators, who submit themselves to Clark's authority. However, in an effort to achieve some checks and balances, Clark submits himself in turn to one of these two men. Under these three heads are 11 coordinators who are in charge of 11 districts. Under the district coordinators are the household heads. All de jure authority in Charismatic communities is male. This is a result of following biblical models of sex roles. There are, however, communites in which one or more females exercise a degree of de facto leadership.

Although there are minor variations on this organizational theme, other Charismatic communities exhibit almost identical patterns of authority. This structural correspondence is due to the influence that the Ann Arbor group has had as a model for those interested in forming their own convenanted communities. Aspiring community leaders engage in frequent visits to Ann Arbor for information and guidance. Seminars on community are given at international conventions where the Ann Arbor group is viewed as the working ideal. Steve Clark's *On Building Christian Communities* is a popular piece of movement literature. Clark also circulated a document in 1973 that explicitly laid out the goals and techniques for achieving a "covenant of a brotherhood." Although Clark's complete document has not been adopted, in particular the section on celibacy, it does detail the general pattern of the ideal of life promoted at Ann Arbor and other covenanted communities.

Of course the covenanted communities contain a small minority of people actually participating in the CCR. For most members the weekly prayer meeting is the hub of movement activity. Each prayer group has its own leaders, who have a great deal of autonomy to organize and determine events to suit themselves. Since there is no centralized control, and no certification procedures are needed to become a prayer group leader, a wide range of leadership styles exist. We have found, however, that it is possible to abstract three types of prayer group leadership, and that groups characterized by these different types exhibit unique properties. At one pole are prayer groups having strong lay leadership. In these groups are influential individuals strongly committed to the ideals of the core leadership described above, which are attitudinally much more independent of conventional church authority than the other two types. These are the groups that are most likely to have formed Christian communities and for whom the CCR is a total way of life. At the opposite pole are prayer groups with relatively strong clerical influence—priests either in key positions of power or those who are influential advisers to laymen in key power positions. These groups are much more firmly attached to traditional church authority. Although members of these groups are also very much committed to the Charismatic Renewal, their emphasis is more on Catholic rather than Christian renewal. Between these two extremes are the many groups with relatively weak lay leadership. These groups may well constitute the numerical majority in the United States. They are generally located in small or medium sized towns and are comprised of loyal Catholics who are seeking a fuller expression of their Christianity, but who also have little intention of completely committing their lives to the CCR. Chapter 7 will include evidence that these three leadership types have markedly different effects on certain attitudes of their constituency.

Again, as in the covenanted communities, males are the preferred authority figures in prayer groups. However, females play a significant part in prayer group leadership generally. Even in groups with ac- knowledged male leadership, certain females may actually dominate the directing of prayer group activities. Leadership is generally granted to those individuals who demonstrate their willingness to devote the re- quired time and effort, the skills necessary to inspire and provide joyful order, and the life style that exemplifies CCR ideals. The emphasis in prayer groups and in convenanted communities is on service as a criteria of leadership.

Summary

When Martin Luther nailed his theses to the door in Wittenberg in 1517, he simply wanted to debate certain theological principles with the leaders of the Roman Catholic Church. From Luther's seemingly inauspi- cious act grew the Protestant Reformation. In 1967 a group of several lay Catholic faculty at Duquesne University met to discuss what they per- ceived as inadequacies in their personal devotional lives. From this equally inauspicious activity has grown a religious movement which today involves thousands of Catholic and Protestant laity and clergy. Both those inside and outside the Catholic pentecostal movement may well recoil at the linking of these two events in the history of the Catholic Church, but it is clear that there is a stirring within Catholicism today which does suggest that possible major modifications in the church's structure and activities are underway. The Protestant Reformation re- sulted in a major and permanent schism within Christianity. The Cath- olic Charismatic Renewal is, on the other hand, clearly *within* the struc- tural features of the church—at the present time. Our research, ne- vertheless, suggests that some features of the CCR emphasize behavior and attitudes that could pose adaptation problems both for the church and the CCR.

The emphasis within Catholic pentacostalism upon the *intrinsic* as- pects of religion as opposed to more *extrinsic* factors is part of a present- day tendency for an increasing number of people to seek assurance and understanding from a transcendental perspective on life. As the seminal research of Gordon Allport and others has indicated, concern with the experiential dimension of religion has always characterized a segment of the religious population. Difficulties in measuring empirically this dimension of religion are well known, but the importance of understanding the behavior of those who emphasize that they have "experienced" God in our day is attested to by those who have researched this expression of religion. Catholic pentecostals constitute one such group.

We are examining the CCR as an example of a social movement occurring within the Roman Catholic Church but having to express much of its activity outside the official structures of the church. While we certainly do not contend that there is nothing distinctive about Catholic pentecostalism, we nevertheless feel that much of what is occurring has theoretical explanations within the sociology of collective behavior. The emergence of groups seeking immediacy in religious experience is not new to the church.

Much criticism has been leveled against work in the sociology of religion as being too church oriented and giving insufficient attention to the expression of religion outside the institutional framework. Others argue that religion is no longer, if it ever was, a motivating force in society. Catholic pentecostals provide a particularly apt illustration of the fact that institutional religion is still a dominant expression of people's religious concerns and may serve as a motivation, but they nevertheless point to the inadequacies of traditional religion to meet the religious needs and aspirations of many who cannot bring themselves to break completely with tradition. The pressures of secularization upon religion are a topic of increasing concern to both theologians and sociologists. These pressures are clearly at work in the CCR. A question of paramount interest concerns the response of those in the institutional church to departures from traditional behavior that may be percieved as no longer sufficient for life in the mid 80s. We therefore give attention to predispositions of the social structure that encourage the emergence of new religious movements offering alternative world views to those apparently disenchanted with secular humanism.

2

An Analytical Scheme
and Its Applications to the CCR

A reality as complex as the Catholic Charismatic Renewal can be approached from many different perspectives, and any single approach to that reality will distort it in some manner. For example, someone steeped in the sociology of religion concerning the church-sect typology might approach the Renewal from a definitional point of view in an attempt to answer the question of what it is. This is essentially what Joseph Fichter did in his 1975 book *The Catholic Cult of the Paraclete*. A personality psychologist might view the CCR as an excellent research site within which to study personality factors that promote attraction to "fringe" groups. Psychoanalytically oriented researchers have often asked this type of question of the religiously committed. The political theorist might want to examine the CCR in the context of a challenge to the power of the conventional church hierarchy. Or the social movement theorist might want to account for the emergence of the CCR by examining various socioenvironmental events that promoted the development of a religious collectivity seriously challenging dominant secular and church values (Smelser, 1963).

The analytical framework we apply to the development of the CCR is well within the boundaries of sociological-social psychological theorizing about the determinants of social movements. However, the major difference between the perspective developed here and the more commonly employed orientations is the emphasis we place on a particular aspect of human motivation and its interaction with the social environment.

Traditional Perspectives on Social Movements

Traditional social movement theorizing involves basically two dominant themes tied to two sociohistorical periods. First, the collective behavior theme (Gamson, 1975) characterizes most social movement theorizing prior to and during the student activist decade of the 1960s. Then the social structural-resource mobilization approach (McCarthy and Zald, 1973) begins its ascendancy toward the end of the 1960s and continues to attain supremacy in the decade of the 70s.

The collective behavior emphasis stresses the importance of various social stressors such as marginality, isolation, and relative deprivation in cognitively and emotionally "setting people up" to become involved in a social movement that promises to provide a renewed sense of identity, pride, meaning, and possibly a tool to wrest concessions from those in power (Turner and Killian, 1972).

Until quite recently, these theories of collective behavior relied heavily on motivational assumptions that emphasized human emotionality and irrationality. Elements of Freudian theory along with a generous sprinkling of social psychological theories stressing imitation and blind conformity permeate the collective behavior literature. Terms such as "contagion," "suggestion," "mass consciousness," "milling," and "mental unity" are not simply tools used to describe and explain but are not-too-subtle indictments of those who dare behave in unconventional ways or who challenge conventional wisdom. A recent psychoanalytic approach to very influential public figures dramatically illustrates this tendency by generously lacing the text with words and phrases such as "a citizenry involuntarily caught up in the process like the victims of a strange disease," "strange hypnoid state," and "strange crippling affliction" (Schiffer, 1973). Even Smelser's (1963) influential "value added" theory assumes that collective behavior is a result of primitive mental processes that he terms "short circuiting."

The Resource Mobilization Approach

Theorizing about political social movements took a dramatic about face in the mid and latter part of the 1960s and early 70s. The activist decade of the 1960s found a substantial number of social scientists either directly involved in civil rights and antiwar demonstrations or in basic sympathy with the goals of the protesters. These scholars' newfound respect for civil disobedience was incongruent with the theories characterizing the socially unconventional as overemotional, suggestible pawns. A growing number of theorists began stressing the continuities between socially conventional problem solving behavior and change-oriented collective behavior (Gamson, 1975; Oberschall, 1973; Tilly, 1964).

The resource mobilization approach to social movements argued that various kinds of social stressors are widespread in any given society at a given time, yet relatively few viable social movements emerge to deal with the source of these discontents. Resource mobilization advocates emphasize the availability of organizational resources such as leadership, control of information networks, and the ability to manipulate the legal system as the keys to successful social movement development. These theorists point out that shared grievances are not even necessary to social movement mobilization if a few dedicated people can muster enough resources to create the impression that some kind of need exists, and thereby garner legal and financial support from societal power structures. In other words, issues can be manufactured by entrepreneurs who know how to manipulate social resources (Perrow, 1979). From this perspective successful social movement cultivation is largely a rational process deliberately engaged in to achieve victory in the arena of conflict over scarce or valued social resources such as money or power.

More recent approaches have sought to combine the stress and the organizational resource orientations to explain more adequately certain modern social movements (Walsh, 1981), and we will construct a variation of that combination. However, the major division in social movement theorizing is still between the older theories picturing movement participants as irrational pawns and the more contemporary theories emphasizing rational decision making as part of the social conflict process.

The increased respectability granted to civil protesters has not been generalized to participants in contemporary religious movements. With the exceptions of Gerlach and Hine (1970), and Bromley and Shupe (1979, 1980), very little has been done to demonstrate the continuities between religious and secular movements from a perspective that does not portray the actors as somewhat unhinged. Social and psychological science in general has displayed ambivalent attitudes toward religious phenomena, and it may be useful to explore briefly the roots of this ambivalence before presenting our own analytical scheme.

Religion as a Sociological and Psychological Focus of Inquiry

Classical sociologists tend to align themselves unabashedly on one of two sides with regard to the role of religion in society. There are those who view the religious response as integral to individual and social functioning (for example, Durkheim, 1912), or as a basic element in social change (for example, Weber, 1930). However, some side with Marx in hoping that secularization will eventually free humankind from the oppressive "religious reflection of the real world" (1936, I:84). Of course Freud's negative view of religion paralleled Marx's notion that religion is the opiate of the people. The secularization theme runs potently through sociological theorizing in general. Even some theologians, such as Cox (1964) and Van Buren (1963), have viewed humankind's separation from religion as a healthy process congruent with God's master plan. From this perspective, intense religiosity is something of a social atavism most likely to be found among those whose world view is somewhat atavistic. Troeltsch tells us, for example, that "it is the lower classes which do the really creative work, forming communities on a genuine religious basis. They alone unite imagination and simplicity of feeling with a non-reflective habit of mind, and an urgent sense of need" (1931:44). Troeltsch's message is unambiguous: genuine religious expression is a product of nonreflective and simple individuals who predominate in the lower classes (Troeltsch was definitely *not* lower class).

There are notable parallels to this type of thinking in the psychology of religion literature. Contemporary religious research disproportionately attempts to establish associations between indexes of religious involvement and activity negatively valued in contemporary society. For example, in a summary article on the psychology of religion, James E. Dittes (1969) discusses the dominant research emphasis, which by and large has sought to demonstrate that religiosity is some function of faulty learning or inadequate socialization. High religiosity has been hypothesized to correlate with low self-esteem, relatively low intelligence, high dependence and suggestibility, and various indexes of poor personality integration.

As Dittes points out, in the 1960s some psychology of religion literature took a different tack and began attempting to link desirable psychological traits and certain aspects of religion. Some psychologists suggested that there may be a significant difference between those who are truly religious and those who are conventionally religious. Indeed the truly religious were reported to be more likely to possess a whole battery of desirable traits than the conventionally religious. They generally displayed greater intelligence, higher levels of education, greater ego strength, more trust, and less authoritarianism than their less fortunate conventional brethren (Allport and Ross, 1967; Keene, 1967).

Social scientists in general view secularization as a somewhat evolutionary sociohistorical process. Max Weber (Gerth and Mills, 1946) borrowed the philosopher Schiller's phrase, "disenchantment of the world," to describe the development of thought patterns from primitive, magical, and mythical forms to the eventual triumph of scientific rationality. While there can be little argument about the fact of secularization as a dominant sociohistorical trend, its long-range implications are far from certain. To link secularization with the eventual disappearance of religion, as do Marx and Freud, involves several assumptions. First, the secularization hypothesis implies a linear trend, even though linear relationships are relatively rare in good science. Even economic trends exhibit wavelike characteristics. Secularization owes its success to the continued demonstration that the scientific method and rational organization are superior methods of human problem solving. Any event or combination of events that creates the perception that the marginal utility of the scientific-rational approach is decreasing could erode support for that perspective. Weber (Gerth and Mills, 1946) clearly thought that situations of stress and ambiguity often revive beliefs in miracles and the transcendent. An increasingly affluent and orderly world may not require religious meaning systems to provide comfort and purpose. A world perceived as in chaos may offer no other useful alternative.

Another unstated assumption that appears to undergird some social scientists' belief in the eventual disappearance of religion is that the dominant religious form must be the monolithic churches, with a sprinkling of sects here and there, which have characterized so much of Western history. Analytically, this and the previous assumption are identical in that they are expressions of a simple trend hypothesis—what has been will be. Although trend hypotheses have been useful in economics, demography, and other social sciences, they also have demonstrated woeful shortcomings in their inability to deal with social change. It is entirely possible that traditional conceptions of religion, and their supporting organizational forms, may change in response to various social pressures. In fact, it would be remarkable if rapid change in the secular sphere did not force change in the realm of the sacred. However, a change in form does not equal extinction.

A final assumption is that macro social science generally provides, when it considers it at all, very complicated assumptions about human motivation. Indeed the very task of constructing macro theories that appear systematic and capable of test requires a substantial degree of both oversimplification and overgeneralization. While such a theory may be attractive because of its ease of comprehension and application, it may also hopelessly distort reality.

Our goal in constructing a theory which will help us order the data we have accumulated on the CCR is to place this particular manifestation of religious behavior squarely in the category of human behavor in general. We are attempting to normalize religious behavior by stressing what it has in common with other types of human behavior. This approach is a result of our extensive interaction with the subjects we set out to study. For example, although we did no psychological assessments of personality dispositions, we did note that the frequency of "odd" types among CCR participants was no greater than the frequency of "odd" types at sociological conventions or Elks Club meetings or any other gathering of large numbers of people. If anything, we would give the edge to most of the CCR participants we have met. This approach to theorizing also arises from our belief that the attempt to delineate categories of behavior (such as religious, deviant, or organizational) has yielded very little in terms of valuable understanding of human behavior. This is one attempt at an integrative approach.

Social Movements as Manifestations of Attempts to Control a Problematic Environment

The analytical scheme developed below explicitly pursues the elements common to all social movement development. We take Cantril's (1941) perspective that social movements of all types are expressions of people's attempts to solve problems using whatever resources are available. To adopt such an approach means that we shall not dwell on the possible differences between religious and political movments but shall emphasize their common elements. The aforementioned tendency to treat religious phenomena as beyond the purview of mundane or secular activities has resulted in a rather static, unparsimonious, and unsystematic approach to theorizing about religious behavior. We hope to redress some of these shortcomings.

Our approach is unabashedly eclectic, freely borrowing elements of value from many sources. The goal is to tie together factors occurring at the societal, small group, interpersonal, and personal levels of analysis. We eventually construct a process model of movement development, both deductively and inductively derived, focusing on information development, receptivity, transmission, and control. Prior to the presentation of the model, however, we need to explicitly discuss the assumptions underlying our image of humankind. All sociological and social psychological theories embody assumptions about the nature of what is under investigation. Some sociologists, such as Talcott Parsons (1951), and most social psychologists (for example, Shaw and Costanzo, 1970) make these assumptions reasonably explicit. However, it is quite common for social scientists to leave these assumptions unstated, and when unstated, to present theories with either naive, extremely oversimplified foundations, or to present theories whose foundations appear to be quite unsystematically constructed (the hodgepodge of literature that is related to functional theory in sociology is an excellent example). Ambiguous or unstated assumptions provide few checks on a theory's internal consistency or its possible levels of generalization.

We begin with the assumption that individuals are capable of self-regulatory, flexible, symbol-mediated behavior. This assumption is compatible with most contemporary orientations in psychology and sociology, including certain strains of behaviorism (Mahoney, 1975; Bandura, 1977). To accept this assumption does not imply that "pure" behavioristic, psychoanalytic, or physiological approaches have nothing of importance to say about human behavior. But it does mean that, in our view, the latter approaches either deal with factors not crucial at a social level of analysis, or with factors that can be more efficiently handled at other levels of analysis.

To assume self-regulatory, flexible, symbol-mediated capabilities does not imply complete autonomy or free will. The within- and between-culture patterning of human behavior is ample testimony to the fact that systematic constraints operate on individuals in ways that circumscribe behavioral options. Self-regulatory, flexible behavior depends on an available repertoire of alternative perspectives that can be used in the decision making process. The availability of and support for these alternatives depends on various circumstances. This is essentially what is being demonstrated in studies relating social class to intelligence levels, academic performance, and varying types of cognitive styles. Furthermore, shared cultural perspectives on behavior determine the type and magnitude of sanctions (reward or punishment) applied to any given behavior. Perceived sanctions influence the probability of the occurrence of any particular kind of behavior (Scott, 1972). These are precisely the underlying asumptions of social role theories, ideas about group and referent-other influence, and socialization theories.

The above assumptions about individual behavior set limits to the means by which social behavior is acquired and directed. They do not, however, say anything about what motivates behavior. Sociologists have long been enamored of various images of the economic human being. People are viewed as essentially acquisitive creatures who prowl about somewhat rationally calculating the relative reward of each act. Although rewards have been defined broadly enough to include symbolic and expressive acts, the major emphasis is on tangible, concrete rewards such as money and the things that money can buy. It is this type of underlying assumption about human motivation that encourages the search for social movement determinants in some sort of absolute or relative deprivation. This underlying assumption about human motivation also promotes the bifurcation of behavior into rational-irrational and instrumental-expressive. Behavior that seems oriented toward the acquisition of some tangible reward, such as a labor group striking for higher wages, is more likely to be classified as both rational and instrumental, while behavior not clearly reward oriented, such as a crowd indiscriminately smashing store windows, is more likely to be viewed as irrational and expressive.

It would be ludicrous to deny the ability of economic forces to shape people's lives. At the same time, there are enough examples dotting the sweep of human history of people choosing austerity over prosperity to cast some doubt on the issue of *homo economicus*. The problem in assuming economic motivation is not that the assumption is in error, but that it is incomplete. The fact that people may be motivated by economic considerations is part of a broader pattern of behavioral dispositions characteristic of all animal behavior oriented toward control of the environment. Economic power is but one means, although certainly a major one, of attaining some measure of environmental control. The behaviorists' notion that money is a generalized reinforcer simply means that it can be used to secure outcomes in many kinds of situations—that is, it is an excellent means of environmental control. The whole of recorded human history can be viewed as an ongoing quest for control: the proliferation of religious systems; the eventual fruition of a reverence for science and technology; the ever-present wars and pogroms, which continue in spite of ancient pleas for love and brotherhood; the increasing global fascination with socialism; the growth of bureaucratic systems of domination; and the trend toward multinational organizations.

At a more micro level, anyone who has watched children develop or has raised animals realizes that conditions which prevent the exercise of control constitute an aversive state to the organism. Both human infants and animals panic when physically restrained. Children raised by overcontrolling parents appear to suffer various kinds of personality pathologies. Anxiety, depression, and even suicide appear to result from attempts to deal with an unmanageable environment.

On the other hand, infants delight in their initial ventures into environmental control such as learning to walk or learning to manipulate doors, drawers, appliances, and other people. Those who stress social rewards and punishments as the sole determinants of children's behavior have apparently never observed that children commonly return again and again to some intrinsically interesting object in spite of consistent punishment for that particular behavior. Systematic research demonstrating that children control their parents to a significant degree is relatively recent despite Erik Erikson's perceptive statement that "a family brings up a baby by being brought up by him." Children of all ages often go to great lengths to establish identities which distinguish them in some ways from parents and peers. The creation of unique identities, along with their supporting activities, provides feelings of efficacy and control. Certain lines of research support the common-sense notion that dating couples occasionally marry primarily as a display of independence against protesting parents. One psychologist (Brehm, 1966) has even developed a theory of behavior based on the idea that people take specific actions to restore or protect perceived threats to their ability to control their own lives.

Our assumptions about human motivation should be obvious at this point. Rather than seeking the genesis of social movements in some "seething cauldron of instincts" or repressed urges buried in the unconscious, some sort of absolute or relative deprivation, some form of over-conformity, or some type of great leader influence, we begin with the assumption that organisms attempt to control their environments. Certainly our position has obvious parallels with Robert White's (1959) notion of competence motivation and, as will become eventually more obvious, with Bandura's (1977) work on self-efficacy. It is also a logical extension of Skinner's (1953) focus on the environment as the source of powerful reinforcers. If the environment is the source of powerful reinforcers, then it is functional for the organism to control that environment to the degree made possible by its own structural capabilities.

However, the assumption that the organism attempts to control its environment must be cast within the framework of our previous assumption that the human organism is a complex symbol user living in a symbolically constructed world. First, in humans, the environment to be controlled includes the self. "One's sense of inner self-esteem derives from experience of self as an active agent of making things actually happen and realizing one's intents in an impartial world" (Franks and Marolla, 1976). The tapestry of human history is laced with innumerable examples of feats of daring, protracted, and painful strenuous athletic activity, extensive personal sacrifice for the sake of exploration and discovery, and the complete expenditure of self for some cause. To assign these types of activities to something like a "need for status" or a "need for social approval" ignores the fact that only a few athletes, daredevils, or martyrs receive any kind of public acclaim during their lifetimes. The reward stems from feelings of efficacy, from having conquered something relatively intractable, including one's self.

Second, the complexity of the above ideas is magnified by the richness of the human information processing system. The ability to relate symbolically to both self and environment means that "it is the expectation, not the objective conditions of controllability" that is important (Seligman, 1975:49). For example, Glass and Singer's (1972) research on control and stress reduction indicates that it it the perception of control that is crucial, and that the perception of control can be created simply by telling the person that they are in control. In attempting to outline the development of a social movement, the task is to delineate the social-environmental conditions which promote definitions of control or their absence, or shape the manner in which strategically located individuals attempt to gain control of an environment defined as somewhat intract-

able. It further follows from the arguments given above that a movement's success and longevity depends on the extent to which it provides
participants with perceptual evidence of increased control.

Third, perceptions of control are notably best supported by overt activity. That is, the primary way that one can know, in the evidential sense,
that one is in control is to bring about some change in the environment
through one's own efforts. This does not mean that feelings of efficacy
cannot be attained vicariously, by watching films or by fantasizing (the
Walter Mitty syndrome), for example. However, such vicarious experiences are probably of more transitory and marginal significance, since
they provide no feedback concerning environmental control. Control is
an attribution of internal causation that is decided after one has somewhat successfully manipulated some part of the environment, including
self. From this perspective struggle, with at least intermittent success, is
preferred over some sort of equilibrium or steady state. Without struggle
of some sort there is no way to attribute control to self. The prevalance
of games in all cultures, the tendency to see devils or conspiracies everywhere, and the universal presence of conflict in all cultures supports the
notion that struggle is in some sense necessary for humans.

Finally, if control is an attribution based on at least partially successful
struggle, then the degree of routinization of a particular activity becomes
an important input into this universal process. The initial solving of a
difficult mathematics problem, the achievement of a long-sought desire,
and the novitiate period of learning a dangerous sport (for example,
skiing) all provide intense pleasure because one has conquered an aspect
of a formerly intractable environment, including one's self. However, the
desired object can only be attained once, the mathematics problem
quickly becomes boring, and the increasingly competent skier must seek
new and steeper slopes or attempt more complex maneuvers in order to
maintain a high level of emotional involvement. The reason that variety
is the spice of life is that perceptions of personal control hinge on activity
that provides evidence of efficacy, and routine activities can only provide
a minimum of such evidence.

Examples of the validity of the above view are virtually endless. For
example, some contemporary women's dissatisfaction with child rearing
and housekeeping may reflect the fact that modern technology and the
proliferation of extrafamilial groups which involve the child very early in
life means that there is little in the housewife role which can provide
feelings of efficacy and control. Common housewives' laments such as "I
am only a can opener and a bus driver" illustrate the destructive aspect
of modern technology in terms of feelings of efficacy, and the frustration
the parent feels at being primarily a transportation medium for children
as they travel from one designated expert (teacher) to another. Technol-

ogy controls most of the services provided in the home, and specialized groups do a major part of socializing the child. The housewife role may be seen as practically devoid of meaningful activities—that is, activities which provide evidence of control. This is in sharp contrast to a time when women grew and processed most of the food that the family ate, helped their husbands in the fields and barns, and passed their attitudes on to their children relatively free of any extrafamilial competition or interference. While the traditional role of women on farms demanded exhausting work, this work was fundamentally tied to the survival of the family. It was meaningful activity because it gave dramatic evidence of efficacy.

One of the destructive aspects of modern technology is that even though it dramatically extends one's control of the environment, it often eliminates activities that give one a sense of control. Similarly, modern systems of specialization remove entire areas of behavior beyond the imagination of most of us and therefore beyond our control. Perhaps those who protest against "the system" are indirectly revealing that people have few activities that provide unequivocal evidence of efficacy. "The system" is not simply the political-business bureaucracy but the entire network of technology and specialization which does such an admirable job of providing services and goods, while at the same time leaving little to challenge the individual's mental or physical abilities.

The Application of the Above Perspective to Religious Phenomena

All religions, indeed all meaning systems, are oriented around themes of order and control: either control of the sociophysical environment or control of self or both. The type of control stressed by a particular religion is very much dependent on the type of sociophysical environment within which the religion is found. For example, some Eastern religions, developing within harsh, recalcitrant physical environments and a rigid social structure, tend to emphasize personal control, and to show their adherents that the individual can transcend the immediate vicissitudes of life through various kinds of contemplative practices or stringent personal disciplines. They teach that one masters the sociophysical environment by rising above it and by placing one's self beyond the need for all but the most basic creature comforts. Fasting and other types of self-imposed deprivations are techniques which allow attributions of self-control and attributions of environmental control; one has transcended the mundane and can now view it in a detached, critical, almost godlike manner. On the other hand, religions which developed in industrializing Europe and the frontier United States emphasized self-control as a complement to environmental mastery, not as a route to transcendence. Industrializing and frontier societies offer many possibilities for external control and unlimited acquisition in the service of God. Calvinists, Quakers, and Mormons all stressed personal control as a complement to environmental mastery. Of course secular ideology, with its worship of technology (the latest religious system), has relatively little use for any stringent system of self-control. Indeed technology does the controlling, and all that is needed as input from increasingly enfeebled human creatures is a bit of maintenance, some replacement, and more development. To achieve feelings of mastery the technocrat can turn to alcohol, drugs, sex, or recreational challenges such as parachuting, hang gliding, or mountain climbing.

Even the secular religionists, or those who attempt to divorce certain religious experience from any notion of God, still stress themes of order and control when attempting to delineate the nature of the transcendent experience. The psychologist Abraham Maslow (1970) lists some of the following characteristics of so called peak experiences:

> the whole universe is perceived as an integrated and unified whole. (theme of order)

> There is tremendous concentration of a kind which does not normally occur. . . . figure and ground are less sharply differentiated. Important and unimportant are also less sharply differentiated, i.e., there is a tendency for things to become equally important rather than to be ranged in a hierarchy from important to quite important. (Unusual power—a power that permits one to rise above the simple reward-cost implications of reality and become more godlike.)

> The peak experience seems to lift us to greater than normal heights so that we can see and percieve in a higher than usual way. We become larger, greater, stronger, bigger, taller people and tend to perceive accordingly. (Indeed godlike)

> In the peak experience there is a very characteristic disorientation in time and space . . . this is like experiencing universality and eternity. (Again, transcending the mundane and becoming godlike.)

> Of course, this (reconciling oneself to evil in the world) is another way of becoming "godlike."

> In peak experiences, the dichotomies, polarities, and conflicts of life tend to be transcended or resolved.

> The person feels himself more than at other times to be responsible, active, the creative center of his own activities and of his own perceptions, more self-determined, more a free agent, with more "free will" than at other times.

In other words, Maslow is convincingly arguing that peak experiences provide attributions of personal control and environmental mastery that are identical to the function served by all religious meaning systems. A number of proponents of the physical fitness cult, notably D. George Sheehan writing about runners (1975), have described bodily activity in mystical-transcendental terms.

Pentecostalism in particular can realistically be defined as a set of practices that increase the probability of attributions of control. The whole pentecostal emphasis on the Holy Spirit and the gifts of the Holy Spirit are set in the context of a newly granted power which permits individuals to better control their environment, including the self. Healing, prophesying, speaking in unknown tongues, interpreting these unknown tongues, wisdom, and so on, all exemplify extended powers and more efficacious behavior. Indeed the pentecostal would agree that it is God working through the individual that is the source of power which provides the ability to heal all sorts of physical and psychical ailments, to reorder spoiled relationships, and to provide renewed energy to set new goals and successfully pursue them. The crucial point is that this power is exercised by and through individuals and is definitely perceived as extending individuals' control over all aspects of their social-physical environment. It provides an exhilarating sense of renewed efficacy. Thus membership in the CCR exhibits parallels to membership in any successful social movement, whether it be the early labor union movement, the coming to power of the communists in the early twentieth-centruy Russia, the beaten Germans who followed a diminutive Austrian house painter in the early 1930s, or the women who became liberated in the United States during the last couple of decades. The conflict that characterizes the formation of any new movement, the perception of being able to do things not possible previously, the perception of having cornered the market on truth, and the set of activities that provide evidence of the movement's validity, all enhance feelings of control and efficacy.

It is significant that social movements with very secular market-type goals often embody religious elements in their activities. One need only reflect on participation by blacks in the civil rights movement, the numerous independence movements in underdeveloped countries, and the relatively recent efforts of people like Caesar Chavez to organize migrant workers in the United States. In fact, an emerging social movement must be "religious" in order to become successful. In other words, it must provide the individual with activities that result in intense feelings of efficacy and transcendence (supremacy over the mundane). Activities that increase feelings of efficacy result in commitment to that group or organization that promotes, teaches, and controls such activities.

Elements in a Model of
Social Movement Development

At this point in our theoretical development we have a complex, self-evaluating, symbol-using creature who acts in ways that permit a sense of personal control. These activities can be expressed in ways reflecting the entire gamut of human behavior: as love, peace, and cooperation, or as hatred, conflict, and competition. What is now required to flesh out our model of social movement development is an explication of the forces which provide direction to our energized creature. Since we assume that the normal human adult world is primarily a definitional, symbolic product, we must specify events that (a) lead people to define themselves as lacking control over valued aspects of their lives, (b) promote and channel search activity designed to reestablish control, (c) result in the adoption of certain behavior patterns and social alliances that constitute the basis of an identifiable movement, and (d) lead to the formation of a particular type of social organization which comprises the fully formed movement.

These points constitute the basic elements in a model of social movement development. They resemble Smelser's (1963) "value added" approach in the sense that each is temporarily prior to and necessary to the other, but the model differs in the assumptions concerning underlying motivation and the particular dynamics that are stressed. Each of these elements requires further explication.

Until recently, most social movement and social change theorists discussed the importance of certain kinds of strain as determinants of the phenomenon they study. Consistent with the motivational assumptions discussed previously, strain is defined as that condition existing when people define themselves as lacking control over valued aspects of their lives. This definition must be juxtaposed against traditional treatments of "strain."

Some sort of economic deprivation is most often cited by scholars as the single most important strain-inducing element in social movement development. Smelser, for example, tells us that "real or anticipated economic deprivation . . . occupies an important place in the initiation of hostile outbursts, reform movements, revolutionary movements, and new sects as well." While Smelser's statement is generally sound, it is also incomplete, as are all theories stressing economic determinism. People who are in no way economically deprived often start social movements, and those who are clearly deprived generally do not start movements. The Oxford Group movement, which captured much popular fancy in the 1920s, was made up almost exclusively of upper middle class individuals. Absolute or relative economic deprivation may promote social movement development, but the connection is far from being a necessary one. The crucial intervening variable is whether or not the economic condition is defined as limiting one's control of what the person defines as rightfully his. Even Karl Marx recognized the importance of a person's definition of the situation when he posited "false consciousness" as that condition which existed when the economically deprived did not realize the limitations of their situation and identified with the values of the upper class. Certainly economic deprivation can set limits on the degree to which people are able to define themselves as having control over values aspects of their lives, but it is this definition that is crucial and not the economic deprivation per se.

Furthermore, stress researchers have made the point that strain of various types and intensities are endemic to life. Stress is a natural concomitant of living and, at moderate levels of intensity, stimulates creativity, growth, and striving. Strain becomes debilitating when the individual comes to believe that there is nothing within his or her power that can be done to cope with, alleviate, or eliminate it. It is at this point in the life of the individual that a serious search for alternatives is made more probable. For example, researchers have noted that many people in industrial societies experience intense psychological trauma around age forty and begin to engage in out-of-role or even bizarre behavior. It is around age forty that some individuals perceive a waning of both physical and intellectual power. In addition, life no longer appears as a journey without end. The struggles that have encompassed one's existence such as education, occupational mobility, child rearing, and keeping the marriage intact are either completed or beginning to appear as unmanageable feats. Certain valued aspects of life take on a random quality, like trying to control one's grown children, and other valued aspects appear unattainable. This is a crisis in the perception of the ability to control one's own life and promotes a search for alternatives. Some seek alternative mates or radically different lifestyles, or achieve brief perceptions of efficacy through the use of alcohol or other drugs. And of course some discover or rediscover religion.

Many strains which could be channeled into a social movement probably exist in any given population at any given time. Social movement scholars generally seek some type of homogeneous strain that appears to characterize a given population at some sociohistorical period, and oftentimes this somewhat univariate modeling does not appear noticeably to violate reality. Economic deprivation is certainly a significant factor in the formation of the early labor union movement, the migrant worker's attempts to organize, the civil rights struggle, and the modern women's movement. However, the danger of seriously distorting a complex reality in the search for single causes is great. The forces that impel people to participate in a neophyte movement may be phenomenologically as diverse as the participants themselves. The individuals comprising a radical feminist group may owe their allegiance to a domineering father, husband, or employer, to a disastrous marriage, or to the feeling that a male-dominated society has drastically limited their achievement of certain valued goals, or to a host of other reasons. A social movement is able to unite people plagued by various situations that appear beyond personal control. In fact, it seems logical to argue that a social movement will be successful to the degree that its symbols (including its leaders) and program have the ability to unite people affected by heterogeneous strains under a perceptual umbrella of increased control over valued results, whatever these may be.

Of course strain, or events which lead people to perceive themselves as lacking control over valued goals, can be dealt with in many ways other than through the mechanism of a social movement. Some individuals simply continue in the same routine and become increasingly depressed; some attempt to recover feelings of efficacy in activities such as recreation, new jobs, a change of scenery, novel sex partners, or through the ingestion of chemicals which affect the perception of efficacy. So, although strain is always found antedating the development of any social movement, it is by no means a necessary determinant of that movement. We will return to the subject of strain in the next chapter.

The seeds of a social movement lie in collective events which create the perception that alternatives are possible. This can occur through the gradual evolution of norms in response to other aspects of sociotechnical change (for example, the increasing demand for women in various sectors of the labor force in conjunction with technical innovations which reduced the value of their role as homemaker), through relatively sudden normative change resulting from legal impositions or natural disasters which completely disrupt the existing order, (for example, the Supreme Court decisions which forced integration in the United States), or through the concerted efforts of innovators who present alternatives in ways that capture the imagination of others. Implicit in this argument is the notion that change oriented behavior is perceived as having some probability of success (heightened efficacy). The intense civil rights activity of the 1960s occurred after it became clear that the federal government had decided actively to protect the rights of certain minorities.

The occurrence of events that promote the perception that alternatives are available and that change oriented behavior has some probability of success results in increased search behavior. People sharing communication networks begin testing tentative solutions to their various problems. This is a premovement stage where small groups, having relatively short life spans and very fluid membership, try one or another set of solutions.

The histories of the genesis of Christianity, of Russian or Chinese Communism, and of the American civil rights and women's rights movements are ample testimony to this phenomena. These various ephemeral groupings usually have quite different definitions of the problem and quite different proposed solutions to the problems. These tentative groupings increase awareness of dissatisfaction among a wider range of social networks and thereby increase the population pool from which recruits can be drawn. Furthermore, they increase the probability that some event will occur which leads people to perceive a dramatic increase in their ability to control their own destinies. Smelser refers to these events as "precipitating factors," but a more accurate descriptive label would be "commitment activities." The discovery of "commitment activities" provides the actual foundation for a successful social movement.

At some juncture during the search behavior sequence it is necessary that some event or events occur which are sufficiently dramatic to unite some of the heterogeneous seeking groups. These events must be interpretable within the framework of increased personal efficacy. Such events are "commitment activities" and can take many forms, for example, a clash with constituted authority. As long as the clash does not result in virtual annihilation of the contending party, it can be viewed from the perspective of heightened efficacy.

Conflict tends to increase perceptions of personal control. A commitment activity may also take the form of a self-sacrificing leader who demonstrates an extreme degree of self-sacrifice and control. Individuals such as Gandhi, Martin Luther King, Jr., and Caesar Chavez inspired others by demonstrating a degree of personal control which elevated them beyond the masses. By identifying with these figures and emulating their activities, one can also increase one's own sense of mastery. Miracles of various kinds can also be commitment devices. The occurrence of highly valued, statistically improbable events during a time of intense seeking can be interpreted as evidence that the behavior patterns making up the seeking activity are useful in bringing blessing from above. Such blessings are dramatic evidence of increased efficacy. Carefully orchestrated mass demonstrations can also be commitment devices. The Nazi mass rallies, with their giant flags, militant music, impressive costumes, and bombastic speeches appeared to provide feelings of increased mastery, especially to a people psychologically whipped by war and inflation. Finally, experiencing situations of somewhat self-imposed personal deprivations can also increase feelings of personal efficacy. As long as the individual perceives the deprivation as self-selected, he or she will interpret it as further evidence of self-mastery and will feel more committed to the group promoting the deprivation-inducing activities. This process of commitment due to deprivation or effort is discussed in the disso-

nance and attribution literature in some detail. Various commitment
activities can occur in combination.

Implied in the above discussion is the existence of common or overlapping communication networks. News of events must be disseminated to
at least some of the preexisting subgroups seeking solutions to problems.
These communication networks can take a number of forms. Probably
the most common are networks available due to proximity (such as a
college campus, prison, or neighborhoods), those due to common media
exposure (television is an excellent example), and those due to preexisting social relationships (friendship shared with people in the adjoining
village, the university fifty miles away, and so on).

Once a commitment activity occurs and is recognized as such, it can
be used to cement individuals into positions of power. Those who recognize the importance of the commitment activities can begin systematically applying them so as to attract and commit others. It is at this
stage during movement development that leadership begins to take definite, patterned forms. We do not intend to imply that emerging leaders
use commitment activities in a Machiavellian manner, although this is
always a possibility. Adolph Hitler certainly organized the Nazi Wag-
nerian pageantry with an eye on its manipulative value. It is highly
probable that most such devices arise serendipitously as people pursue
alternative perspectives through trial and error behavior. The point is
that a social movement becomes recognizable as such and takes on
definite organizational form when emerging leaders begin systematically
applying commitment devices which have demonstrated their ability to
attract and hold others and to unify diverse subgroups.

This initial cadre of the now recognizable movement comprises the
elite core. From this core will come future staff members and leaders as
the movement broadens its scope of application. From this core emerges
the movement's cultural heroes. They are heroes in the sense that they
are the ones who experienced the initial struggle and the search, and
who discovered, or had revealed to them, the commitment activities. As
the movement takes on a more rigid, institutionalized structure, these
core people will be the primary instruments shaping that structure. In
fact the thrust toward structure is primarily a thrust toward refining and
preserving the commitment activities. In time, if the movement persists,
the commitment activities will take on a ritual quality.

However, once an inital core of devotees have accumulated around
commitment activities, a final stage remains in the evolution of a social
movement. A truly successful social movement must broaden its base of
attraction and not engage in behavior that would bring about its annihilation or destroy its credibility. In other words, it must promote its
claims to legitimacy. To do this, movement leaders must devote consid-

erable time and effort to the art of impression management. Goffman (1959) discusses impression management at the interpersonal level at great length. Successful impression management revolves primarily around the task of demonstrating to a wider audience that the movement does increase their ability to control their own destinies, while concomitantly demonstrating that the movement's activities are in line with or are more perfect examples of already existing values. For example, both labor unions and civil rights movements faced the dual task of convincing potential members that the movement's programs would increase their ability to realize desired results, and of convincing at least some segments of the power structure that the movement's program was oriented toward valued goals such as brotherhood and democracy. Only after a movement has successfully gone through the impression management stage can it realistically hope to challenge or overturn the existing power structure. Because, if it has successfully managed impressions, it has broadened its base of attraction considerably and has also coopted members of the traditional power structure.

The relationship of this model to the resource mobilization approach to social movements is quite obvious. However, it deviates dramatically from that perspective in its attempt to answer the question of why: why some attempts to mobilize and organize people succeed while many or most fail; why some movements last a year, some a generation, some even longer; why individuals are willing to invest enormous resources in some movements, while other movements exact minimum amounts of time, talent, and energy. The key to answering these various questions is the assumption that increased perception of control is the mediating factor that makes all the organizational-institutional elements work. Traditional sociological correlates of social movement development, such as status inconsistency, social isolation, relative deprivation, and rising expectations, are all indexes of perceived helplessness or lack of control. Social movements succeed to the degree that these perceptions are changed due to involvement in movement activities, especially activities that we label "commitment devices" (Gerlach and Hine, 1970).

Summary

Attempts to explain any social movement can borrow from several theoretical orientations. Two major perspectives characterize modern sociological and social psychological theorizing: the collective behavior and the resource mobilization approaches. The collective behavior approach tends to emphasize the social psychological states of individuals, while the resource mobilization approach focuses on social structural conditions that favor movement formation. The former theory pictures

Figure 2 General Stages of Social Movement Evolution.

1. Events which erode traditional perspectives and promote perceptions of helplessness, meaninglessness, and worthlessness.

2. Events which strengthen the perception that options are available and that change oriented behavior has some possibility of success. (Heightened perceptions of efficacy.)

3. Search behavior and the formation of multiple premovement groups within the structure of overlapping social networks.

   Tentative Solution 1
   Tentative Solution 2
   Tentative Solution 3
   .
   .
   .
   .
   Tentative Solution N

4. The discovery of commitment techniques or externally imposed commitment events (e.g., political oppression or violence).

5. Leadership consolidation and the beginning of movement structure using the commitment techniques.

6. Increasingly claims to legitimacy through impression management, co-optation of important or high status individuals, and the growth of membership. This is the "success" stage.

people as primarily emotional creatures, while the latter approach emphasizes rationality and enlightened self-interest.

Because social scientists generally view religious behavior as primarily emotional in nature, there have been few attempts to apply resource mobilization theory to religious movements. We argue that what appears as primarily emotion-driven behavior can have some very rational, goal directed purposes. Heightened emotion can be viewed as a resource that enhances group effectiveness. We try to demonstrate the applicability of resource mobilization theory to the CCR and other modern religious movements.

However, we also view certain aspects of human motivation as crucial to understanding participation in modern religious movements. The recent attention given to perceived efficacy and perceptions of control in the social psychology literature seems particularly appropriate when applied to the functions served by modern religious movements for the educated middle class who comprise the bulk of their membership. The rapidity of social change characterizing the last two decades of American life has eroded the perception of many people that they have control over important aspects of their lives. Social movements, such as the CCR, which restore this perception of control will probably be successful in attracting and holding members.

3
Social Strains and the Development of the CCR

Strain, as a phenomenon of all life forms, is a part of social movements, though strain does not directly determine new activities and perspectives. Strains of various types are a dominant feature of being a reactive creature in a responsive environment rather than an occasional rent in the fabric of life. Strains may be simply endured; they may lead to apathy, depression, or other forms of withdrawal; or they can lead to search behavior, which may take many possible forms. Some search behavior may lead to the development or discovery of innovative behavior. If these innovations provide heightened perceptions of efficacy, and if there exists some type of preexisting communication network through which news of the innovation may travel, then a social movement may possibly take root. The link between strains and social movements is very indirect, very much subject to definitional, trial and error behavior, and highly dependent on social-environmental events which promote the perception that alternatives are possible.

No single set of strains affects all segments of a social movement. In one sense a social movement can be viewed as an alignment of somewhat heterogeneous groups which are laboring under a number of distinct but interrelated problems. This is especially true for those types of movements social scientists refer to as "expressive" movements: those characterized by outpourings of intense emotions. In discussing social strains that eventuated in the CCR, we can identify three general sets of problems. First, there are problems that emanate from the very structure of the Catholic Church. These primarily concern relationships between the church and its members, the church and non-Catholic Christians, and the church and secular society in general. Second, a number of social problems captured the awareness of certain segments of the

American public in the period just preceding the emergence of the CCR. The mass media, including elements of the Catholic press, created the impression that reality consisted primarily of the war in Southeast Asia, various manifestations of institutional racism, and the persistence of poverty in the most affluent country that ever existed. Third, tensions generated by problems in living that appear chronic in modern industrial society also contributed to what eventually became the CCR. Feelings of meaninglessness, unstable interpersonal relationships, and other factors that aggravate a sense of inefficacy are reflected in the testimonies of many members.

Clearly, these multifaced problems did not affect each participant in the same manner or to the same degree. Different pools of individuals became involved in somewhat distinct matrices of strains. We reject monocausal approaches that attempt to link complex social movements to some type of single, shared strain. Specific segments of a population must be tied to specific strains in order to approach an adequate analysis. This will be attempted with each of the classes of strain identified above.

Strains Resulting from Church Structure

It is impossible to read many pages of CCR literature without finding mention of the Second Vatican Council called by Pope John XXIII to deal explicitly with various issues of church renewal. It would be a serious mistake, however, to assume that the impetus for the CCR began with the strains articulated and debated at that council. The Second Vatican Council was a response to some long-standing pressure which had recently been defined as reaching crisis proportions. One master theme dominates the Catholic literature prior to Vatican II: how can the church adapt to, and survive the challenges posed by various facets of secular humanism? This theme was actually composed of a number of subissues. First, in the realm of theology the question was how to reconcile the findings of modern science, the image of human beings posed by Freudian psychoanalysis, and the increasing impact of existential philosophy with the intellectualized, frozen theology still dominant in the Roman Curia. Second, in terms of organizational structure, the perennial problem of centralized authority appeared even more acute as the socialistic-democratic ethic spread throughout the world. Third, questions of moral obligation centered on the reluctance of the offical church to take activist stands on issues that consumed modern liberals: racial oppression, poverty, and colonial types of war and domination. Finally, an overriding concern was the survival of the church, indeed of Christianity itself, in an increasingly hostile world. The fragmentation of Christianity had been increasingly recognized as a self-defeating defensive strategy by both Protestant and Catholic leaders. For the highly involved, informed, and committed Roman Catholic, the assumptive world appeared to be disintegrating. Some type of reform appeared necessary to detour the church from its self-selected road to destruction.

Each of the issues outlined above could be posed in terms of a progressive versus a conservative point of view, and this is eventually the form they took at the Vatican Council discussions. A brief explication of each of these issues will set the stage for a subsequent discussion of Vatican II and its role in the formation of what was to eventually become the CCR. The immediate issue concerns those events that led committed, informed Catholics to perceive a loss of control over the eventual fate of the church and Christianity in general.

It was the catastrophe of the Second World War that gave progressive Catholic theology a real "shot in the arm."[1] The Nazi phenomenon demonstrated in a dramatic way the potential of people for violence and for apparently uncritical conformity to authority. Many of those involved in implementing the Nazi destruction blueprint were Christians, including Roman Catholics. Furthermore, the offical church position on the German atrocities was at best ambiguous. Since Europeans were the tragic recipients of the worst of the Nazi legacy, it should come as no surprise that the war's greatest impact on theology occurred in Europe. A contingency of Catholic theologians emerged from the ashes of postwar Europe asking fundamental questions about the nature of authority and the extent of the individual's allegiance to constituted authority. It is also important to understand that European theologians, especially the French, dominated Catholic theology in the mid-twentieth century (Tavard, 1967:15–16).

The issues posed by these theologians revolved around the importance of historic relativism and existential philosophy for modern Catholic theology. The dominant thrust of Catholic theology since Thomas Aquinas has been a form of scholasticism. This is a view of theology as primarily the realm of experts schooled in Aristotelian methods of reasoning and argumentation. Theology is a search for absolutes and these eventually become dictates handed down to the laity. In this type of system Scripture is a reference work to be used by the cleric, not a means of permitting the rank and file to experience the word of God. Such an approach to theology befits a highly centralized organization attempting to defend itself against "foreign" ideas.

Historical relativism and existentialism posed serious challenges for

---

[1]We acknowledge our debt to Edward Walsh for his valuable insights concerning material discussed in this section.

dogmatic theology. Their challenges were made viable by the Nazi atrocities. These two philosophical schools resurrected the notion that each age must reinterpret its theology in light of its own peculiar realities. Historical relativism, especially the Hegelian and Marxian varieties, raised again the possibility that theological views were a function of social and economic events characterizing a given era. The relative inaction of the churches in Nazi Germany suggested that this particular view had a great deal of inductive validity. The implication of that possibility was clear: it was time to take a fresh look at the prevailing definitions of people's relationship to God and to the church in light of modern philosophy and science. The theologian-scientist Teilhard de Chardin had already presented a model which integrated science and theology. It appeared to be simply a matter of time until someone did the same for modern philosophy. (See especially Teilhard deChardin's *The Phenomenon of Man*, 1959.)

Existentialism was the philosophical perspective which attracted the most attention among progressive European theologians. Existentialism complemented historical relativism in its depiction of life as an ongoing, ever-changing stream of events. From this viewpoint there can be no dogma that will permit adaptation to existing reality. Authoritatively dictated precepts ignore the experiential dimension of life and the fact that the individual is faced with choices that demand the assumption of personal responsibility beyond that which can be guided by such abstract principles. Existentialism emphasizes the individual and his or her experiences and the necessity for personal choice based on intelligent reflection on that experience. And largely as a reaction to the Nazi terror, existentialism was a denunciation of institutionalism and centralized control.

The thrust of theology emanating from the European progressive thinkers was clear: the church must open itself to the world. Specifically, it must deemphasize the institution and reemphasize the individual and his or her relationship to God; it must realize that the sacraments are not the sole (nor always the most important) means of uniting people and God, but that God can be directly experienced by the prayerful individual; and that Scripture should be redefined as the word of God speaking directly to the person and not simply a resource book to be used by the religious elite. A preoccupation with the church was to give way to a preoccupation with God and Christ—Christianity as lived by a body of believers, not as a frozen institutional edifice.

Of course church fathers could not ignore these revisionist ideas. The papal encyclical *Humani Generis* (1960) was an explicit attempt to temper the progressives and reemphasize exactly where the power to define theological reality lay. Some of these progressive theologians—Henri deLubac and Yves Congar, for example—were prohibited from further teaching and publishing. However, these ideas also had their supporters among progressive elements in the hierarchy who would eventually have a substantial impact in the deliberations of Vatican II. Of special note among these modernist ecclesiastics is Cardinal Leo Suenens of Malines-Brussels, Belgium. Not only did Suenens play a key part in realizing the progressives' goals at the Second Vatican Council, he was also to be the first highly placed cleric to publicly support the CCR.

Another related source of post-World War II strain within the Roman Catholic Church was the increasingly vocal criticism generated by an expanding Catholic political left. The political left had never occupied a place of influence in the institutional church. It is primarily in the early and mid 1960s that the Catholic left becomes unabashedly outspoken about the discontent with intransigent church structure and with the church's relative lack of involvement in the great liberal issues of that period (Colaianni, 1968).

Prior to Vatican II some church officials were becoming aware that they were losing the international struggle for people's souls with various strains of secular humanism. Communist and socialist ideology and practice tackled the plight of the downtrodden head-on, and offered what appeared to be realistic promises of a future when the meek would indeed inherit the earth. The church's long-standing abhorrence of atheistic communism was clearly stated in Pope Pius XI's encyclical of 1937, *On Atheistic Communism*, which was viewed as a quashing of the Catholic political left. However, secular humanism continued to capture the fancy of many dedicated Christians precisely because it appeared to be a more effective means to bring about a more just world order than did the wait-and-pray method offered by the traditional churches. It is hardly surprising that some protest movements became labeled as more Christ-like than those churches that appeared to ignore burning contemporary issues.

But these theological-moral issues did not affect the vast bulk of those persons identifying themselves as Roman Catholics. These conflicts were of intense interest to a highly educated, deeply involved elite to be found primarily in seminaries and other centers of Catholic higher education in both Europe and the United States. To this elite it appeared increasingly obvious that the church's intransigence made it irrelevant and that this irrelevance would eventually spell its demise. The church appeared futile compared to various strains of secular humanism, and this perception of a loss of efficacy was indeed acute among this segment of Roman Catholics.

The Impact of Secular Humanist Beliefs

To say that these great theological and moral debates did not reach the
average parishioner is not to imply that secular humanism was not
having some impact on them also. Ideology seldom inflames the majority. What concerns most people are those events that impinge on them as
they conduct their daily lives. The ethical trend toward greater personal
freedom found a concrete expression among many Catholics in terms of
the perennial birth control controversy. The question of church authority
was most vulnerable at the point at which the church continued to
dictate sexual behavior for married couples. Advances in birth control
technology, successful education about population problems, and the
increasingly popular definition of sexual behavior as an issue to be decided by participants gave many Catholics the idea that this was something to be controlled by them and not the church. As an increasing
number of Roman Catholics began using officially disapproved contra-
ceptive techniques, they were taking a significant step away from control
by constituted authority. The erosion of allegiance to authority in this
particular sphere was bound to lead to a general credibility crisis. The
increasingly dramatic decline in church attendance by Roman Catholics
seemed further evidence that the church was approaching an acute state
of powerlessness. One merely has to skim the pages of Catholic publications in the decade of the 60s to see the intense preoccupation with
questions of church authority, individual freedom, and potential alternatives to existing hierarchical arrangements. For example, the September
1965 issue of *The Catholic World* has five articles devoted to "The Christian and Religious Liberty"; a September 1966 article discusses "Liberty
within the Catholic Church"; a November 1967 article deals with reform
of canon law in such a way to promote personal freedom. This same
publication also dealt extensively with the birth control controversy. In
the July 1964 issue Cardinal Suenens is cited as stating that medical
research is close to perfecting a morally acceptable pill that may be used
for family planning. Of course this possibility was never realized. There
is little question, however, that the church had lost much of its ability to
provide its members with feelings of worth and efficacy relative to competing philosophical viewpoints. Secular humanism had pervaded the
edifice at every level.

The American Catholic Church had long been characterized as an
ethnic church (Greeley, 1972). One of its most important functions was
to provide psychic support and social services to those Catholic ethnics
who had not yet been assimilated into the dominant structure of power
and influence in America. In many urban areas, Catholic parishes took

on ghetto characteristics as they became constituted of primarily Irish, Polish, or some other Eastern European ethnic group. But as these various ethnic groups became increasingly mobile, both horizontally and vertically, their community structures disintegrated and their need for church support lessened. Again the church lost its ability to provide feelings of efficacy to another part of its membership beyond that provided by secular organizations and ideologies. This is simply one further increment to its growing powerlessness. Leaders of the CCR are well aware of this fact and have commented on it extensively (S.B. Clark, 1972a; Martin, 1971).

Problems of demystification and loss of function are pandemic in modern churchdom. Modern churches, especially the more progressive Protestant varieties, led the way in abolishing impressive display and rituals, feared and respected authority structures, and dogmatic pronouncement about the proper way for Christians to live their lives. Sin became something an enlightened pastor only mentioned in the context of a joke. Even God became something of an embarrassment to discuss in any but an extremely abstract way.

The outcome of this modernization trend, besides the more obvious democratization thrust, was a complete loss of anything that generates a sense of awe and devotion—those things so crucial in initiating and maintaining commitment to any ideology or organization. Certainly the human attraction to awe- and mystery-inspiring activities did not pass with the abolition of medieval church practices: witness the Russian, Chinese, and Cuban revolutions with their panoply of saints, their various "bibles," their uncompromising ideologies and dogmatic authorities, their demands for self-sacrifice and self-perfection in the service of a greater cause, and their destruction of heretics. The preoccupation of some secularists with drug experiences of various kinds, with sexual orgasm, and with the perfection of self through sport could be viewed in the context of attempts to recapture that sense of mystery and transcendent meaning that religion provided in the past. See Cox, *The Feast of Fools* (1971) for a possible countertrend here.

In their attempts to find new ways to attract and hold parishioners the modern churches tried various management and marketing promotion techniques. Troubled parishioners were offered the latest fad in psychotherapy or semistructured group therapy. If young people became excited by issues of racial justice, colonial wars, and sexual freedom, then these became the cause célèbre of the churches. Indeed the latest secular-humanist preoccupation has tended to be interpreted as a concrete manifestation of the will of God. This is part of what has been referred to as an identity crisis in the churches. In other words, the churches no longer provide anything distinctive to help people manage their existence beyond those services and philosophies offered by the secular humanists. In this atmosphere religion loses any distinctive cultural characteristics and becomes an appendage to dominant secular institutions. Indeed, the primary function of the modern church may well be that of providing ecclesiastical blessings to the dominant secular ideology of the day.

Many Catholics viewed post-Vatican II events as indicating that the Roman Catholic Church was in the throes of its own reformation. It appeared that authority and dogma were being deemphasized; the "new" liturgy replaced the centuries-old Latin rituals with folk and rock music and a "one of the boys" view of the priest; and the impression was created that to be concerned about one's fellow human beings was the sole essence of Christianity. The effects of this change in Catholics' definition of the situation are still shaking the edifice. Vocations to the priesthood have fallen off dramatically (with a partial revival in the last two years); vocations to the nunnery have experienced significant declines; and some priests and laypeople are demanding the right to construct their own morality, while others are retreating to a more comfortable medievalism and arch-conservatism.

All of the problems discussed above can be interpreted as a crisis in the church's ability to provide the individual with feelings of efficacy. Contemporary philosophy, supported by a technology and economy that makes the philosophy workable, emphasizes the individual's autonomy and freedom. Each individual can make choices quite independent of church dogma without any real negative consequences. Without a cohesive community of believers to back up dogma with sanctions, individual deviations go unpunished and further autonomy is reinforced. The Irish, Italian, and Slovak Catholics in the United States no longer need the church to provide social contacts leading to jobs, no longer require the protection afforded by a religious-ethnic education, and no longer need the welfare services provided by church groups. Secular institutions serve these functions much more effectively; secular machine and human technology also appear to increase individual efficacy beyond that provided by a religious approach to problem solving. If psychoanalysis appears to solve personal problems of guilt and depression, then sacraments like confession lose much of their function (or if the culture has defined guilt away, then confession is also passé). If miracles no longer occur, then the individual turns to that secular professional who is defined as able to assist him or her. In other words, from many different perspectives the church can be viewed as an institution that has lost the ability to provide the individual with perceptions of efficacy. In the language of traditional sociology, it has become a functionless institution.

Strains in the Secular Sphere I:
The Great Social Experiment of the 60s

The decade of the 1960s witnessed a coalescing of factors that would eventually create a pool of disillusioned young people who would reject social action as a human problem solving technique and who would seek alternatives that appeared to have greater power. Again these events affected primarily one subgroup—college students from the established middle and upper middle classes who were influenced by the events described below.

Unlike their European counterparts, American college students do not have a dramatic history of sociopolitical activisim. There are many possible reasons for this relative lack of involvement. Prominent among them is that somewhat different functions are served by higher education in Europe and the United States. During the expansionary and secularizing period of higher education in the United States, it became clear that higher education was becoming a major route of upward mobility for, initially, the lower middle class and later the working class. In Europe, however, higher education has been primarily a straigthforward adjunct to a clearly class based society; children of established families comprise the vast bulk of the European college population.

Having one's roots in an established, secure background versus a background characterized by struggle and uncertainly is likely to affect one's perceived behavioral options. The talented lower middle or working class youth who is using the university system as a springboard to a professional or managerial career has to make a major commitment to the dominant institutional and societal values. In other words, these youths must "keep their nose clean." Any activity which indicated anything but complete allegiance to upper middle class ethical and economic values, such as a prison record resulting from social protest, threatens the youth's successful swim up the prestige stream. On the other hand, this type of student may engage in so-called "expressive" behavior, such as swallowing goldfish, panty raiding, and so on, since these are defined as transitory and as indicating no disaffection with dominant middle class values. However, the European student may risk institutional rejection, since he or she has family connections to fall back upon which virtually ensure a comfortable future.

The affluence engendered by the post-World War II baby boom and other postwar stimuli to American industry substantially modified the situation depicted above. A mass of students began entering college in the 1950s and 60s who had been reared in relatively affluent, secure families. Their primary goal was not to surpass their parents' occupational status, since many of their parents were already professional or semiprofessional types. These students expected somewhat automatically to inherit a prestigious occupation because it seemed to be the natural order of things. No longer did students feel that they had to worry excessively about treading the straight and narrow in order to attain eventually a secure future. Like their European counterparts, these American students did not see economic and social disaster as a likely result of behavior expressing dissatisfaction with the established order.

Furthermore, many of these young people recognized that their parents' hard fought struggle for economic and social betterment had not ensured concomitant increments in personal happiness, sensitivity to the problems of others, family stability, or meaningful social relationships. The so-called hippy movement was designed to be a dramatic repudiation of conventional middle class values. This group of students had relatively high feelings of efficacy. Their entire upbringing in security and affluence reinforced feelings that the world was theirs to shape as they saw fit.

Factors other than affluence also reinforced perceptions of efficacy in this group of young people. The civil rights movement gained momentum from the mid 1950s through the 60s. Middle class white students primarily from northeastern colleges and universities traveled south to join the civil rights activists. Various decisions by the federal government gave the activists impressive victories in their battle against racial discrimination. Widespread and sympathetic media coverage transmitted the images of self-sacrificing but victorious students across the land. It seemed increasingly possible to manipulate the social order by the simple mechanism of well-intentioned citizens collectively taking to the streets. The Vietnam antiwar movement would eventually evolve and be led by many of these same young people who had received their baptism of fire in civil rights protests.

Still other factors promoted the spirit of efficacy that characterized the Catholic and non-Catholic college youth of the 1960s. A number of leaders appeared on the political and religious scene who were able to generate inspiration by their own personal life styles, by their eloquent speeches, by their examples of self-sacrifice in the service of higher values, and by their socially oriented programs. Martin Marty comments on this point most eloquently: "One side of the secular theology turned out to be romantic. In the early 1960s the empirical situation seemed to favor it; Utopia was not wholly implausible. Pope John and President John, Saint Nikita and Reverend King would help take care of things." (Marty, 1968). Eventually President Lyndon Johnson would condense these dreams in his programatic catchword, "the great society."

During this same period other forces were at work within the university communities to reinforce the notion that personal and social ills could be solved through collective efforts. The 1960s witnessed the fruition of what is generally known as the Sensitivity Training or the Encounter Group movement (Back, 1972). Proponents of these techniques succeeded in convincing an increasing number of young people that the way out of problems of identity formation (meaning), ephemeral and unstable social relationships, loneliness, and other personal-social crises was through group sharing, criticism, and guidance. Various types of contrived group experiences increasingly assumed functions that had been provided by religious institutions in the past. "In its drifting away from strictly scientific procedures it (sensitivity training) assumed the religious function of providing a consistent world view and some of the emotional aspects and control of religious ritual" (Back, 1972:19).

There is no question that the eventual founders of the CCR, and its earliest members, were disproportionately represented by politically liberal views which mirrored those of their contemporaries. There is also no doubt that they had visions of a more just world order to be created by their collective endeavors. Both Steve Clark and Ralph Martin were heavily involved in the Cursillo movement (see chapter 4 for a detailed description of this movement) when, at their Sixth National Conference, they came out strongly in favor of various civil rights programs, and the nuclear test ban treaty, and against Barry Goldwater, an extreme conservative, who was running for president. Several issues of *New Covenant,* which in 1972 was designated as "The Monthly Magazine of the Catholic Charismatic Renewal," presented extensive discussions of problems of war, racial justice, poverty, international relations, and social change. In these issues one can find favorable mention of revolutionaries like Che Guevera, Martin Luther King, and Karl Marx. Several articles strongly support some form of socialism as a cure for social problems. Furthermore, our own data on almost 1,000 participants in the CCR demonstrates their very liberal stands on issues such as the Vietnam War and poverty (Bord and Faulkner, 1975). We interviewed group leaders, several of whom had participated in the now famous Duquesne weekend (see chapter 2), and found that they too had been involved in civil rights activities, community work for the socially and physically handicapped, and other programs designed to help the downtrodden. They shared their contemporaries' vision of a just world order which appeared capable of realization in the near future through social action techniques.

However, various events began chipping away at the foundation of this liberal dream. It is difficult to pinpoint a single event which began the slide toward disillusionment with social activism, but certainly the assassination of President John F. Kennedy, and later of his brother, Robert, and Martin Luther King, Jr., shook the assumptive world of the young dreamers, especially that of young Roman Catholic dreamers. In addition, the seemingly endless war in Southeast Asia slowly sapped the enthusiasm of those who thought they were ushers of an improved world order. The National Guard shooting of the students at Kent State University and the police riots at the 1968 Democratic National Convention further highlighted the recalcitrance and ruthlessness of those who represented the established order. In addition to these cracks in the dream, many young idealists who had been working at the community level began to realize that problems of poverty, mental retardation, prison reforms, and individual rehabilitation were extremely resistant to short-term change. During one 2 A.M. conversation over coffee and doughnuts with a married couple who had participated in the Duquesne weekend and were now heading a large, successful prayer group, the issue of disillusionment was dramatically illustrated. They had thought that social activism was the answer to everything. Both had worked with derelicts in Pittsburgh for over three years, but all of their efforts seemed to amount to nothing. The poor were still poor, and the drunks still wanted their bottles.

In a document that was eventually distributed to some prayer groups in the northeastern United States, this disillusionment with secular methods of societal perfection is dramatized by an invidious comparison between powerless pretentious "Humanism" and the "Kerygma of Jesus Christ." Humanism, or counterfeit Kerygma, is depicted as involving "Good works expected to flow from old nature and save self and society." "Man already is 'God' without Jesus salvation or personally receiving the power of the Holy Spirit. . . . Thus power is also within man. Man himself is thus a kind of god. . . . Man not a sinner—rather he is full of hidden power to know hidden things and control nature and other people in remote ways." In other words, the belief that people can build a better world order using their own rationality came to be seen as an illusion. The people who helped spearhead the CCR knew it was an illusion because they had tried it and found it wanting. The great social experiment was defined as a failure.

Strains in the Secular Sphere II: Cognitive Chaos and the Middle Class

We have called attention to the relatively high levels of education achieved by CCR participants. Most of its members, at least through 1973, had at least some college experience. It is quite possible that the growth of the CCR since 1973 has somewhat leveled the degree of educational achievement of the average member. However, it appears to remain very much a middle class movement. Clearly working class Americans are not flocking to prayer meetings and covenanted communities. One of the things we continually attend to in our more recent visits to prayer groups and CCR related conventions is evidence of participants being involved in hard, dirty work. We look for things like "beat-up" hands, stained finger nails, callouses, and conversations indicating assembly line or mechanical work and the like. Such evidence is extremely rare.

It may well be that specific aspects of the educational experience itself resulted, and perhaps are still resulting, in feelings of helplessness. In the mid 1960s "gloom and doom" books such as Paul Ehrlich's *Population Bomb* and Rachael Carson's *Silent Spring* became rather routine reading in most college curricula. During this time the ecology crisis began to be systematically defined and to take on the characteristics of a full-fledged social movement. Threats of nuclear holocuast; the "population explosion" with accompanying images of starvation, increased crime, and debilitating crowding; the continual poisoning of our environment; and other potential catastrophes are continually presented as definitions of the situation to college students who too often do not have the wisdom to realize that all of these issues involve strong elements of opinion and are not ineluctable truth.

Of course, giving attention to social problems during the educational process is not unique to the last decade of modern education. What is unique, is the sense of failure or stagnation in which they are often discussed, and the degree of complexity they involve. The "population bomb" advocates tell us that unless we quickly and radically reduce population growth, the future is indeed ominous. In the next breath we are told that the chances of achieving the desired reduction is almost zero. The ecologists predict dire results unless we take immediate steps to stop air, water, and soil pollutions of various kinds and also act quickly to clean up the mess we have already made. Yet the clean-up process itself is fraught with costs: predictions of business slowdowns with high unemployment and economic collapse; an inability to adequately control insect pests and plant disease; a drastic curtailment in the use of fossil fuels, which involves a dramatic retrenchment in current life styles defined as desirable.

Again, since the crucial point is not actual helplessness itself but definitions of the situation as helpless, some portion of the educated middle class turned back to techniques of environmental control that their relatively helpless ancestors had used—supplication to deities. It is precisely the educated middle class who are being taught a hopeless view of the future. That some of them should turn to beliefs in devils, beliefs that complex problems can be solved by something as simple and effortless as prayer, beliefs that an ancient document has the answer to all problems, and beliefs that we are being watched over by a loving creator is understandable. It is also understandable that this same segment of the population should show an increase in alcoholism and other forms of withdrawal using drugs, frenetic sex, decisions not to form permanent commitments or have children, Eastern religions, and radical communal living. Inevitably, as these pessimistic prophecies filter down into the secondary schools via teachers who learned them in college, younger people began to use the same methods of withdrawal as their elders.

Personal Tensions as a Source of Strain

People throughout the ages have lived under conditions of chronic strain, which renders them open to social experiences giving promise of amelioration. This class of strain generally involves problems in interpersonal relationships and personal health problems not easily dealt with given the existing knowledge base. As discussed in chapter 2, these are problems in what Chapple (1970) has called "the fundamental crises of existence." The tenacity of these crises of existence is attested to by the variety and omnipresence of therapies, counselors, self-help guides, and quack medicine.

The outstanding characteristic of this class of strain is intense feelings of helplessness. The list of specifics include long-standing marital difficulties, a lack of ability to control one's children, an inability to form meaningful friendships, feelings of being trapped through chronic drug use, and acute debilitating health problems such as terminal cancer, crippling arthritis, loss of visual and audio activity, and others.

The importance of these personal strains in providing members for the CCR is amply attested to by the hundreds of testimonies we have either read or heard. A representative sample of these testimonies follows:

> A 47-year-old florist (male): "My wife and I hadn't been getting along for almost three years now. Two of my three sons were on drugs or booze. I was active in a number of parish organizations but none of these activities brought peace or provided us with effective guidelines for living."

> A 20-year-old university student (female): "When I came to college I tried everything: drugs, sex, the whole bit. After a while nothing seemed worth anything. I didn't have any real friends and I was headed nowhere."

> A 38-year-old housewife confined to a wheelchair: "Ever since the accident five years ago I haven't been able to walk. I felt like a nothing. Couldn't be a wife and a mother the way I'm supposed to be. Life seemed useless and not worth living."

> A 46-year-old engineer (male): "My marriage was a mess. Our family never communicated and I spent a lot of time drinking with the boys. My

wife talked about leaving me and God knows she had good reason to. I just quit."

A 23-year-old water tester for a municipal water treatment center (male): "I started smoking dope in high school, really got into it in college, and then started trying all kinds of pills. It got to the point where I didn't know who I was and, for that matter, didn't really care. My parents didn't want anything to do with me, my girl left me, and the only friends I had were the people I'd trip with. Toward the end I kept thinking about blowing my brains out—even got a gun and would stare at it for hours."

A 42-year-old accountant (male): "I've worked for (X) company for 12 years. My supervisor never got off my back and he made it near impossible for me to move up the ladder. Took up drinking and chasing around a little but that just made things worse. Got to where my wife just put up with me. We hadn't said a kind word to each other in months. Nothing seemed to work anymore."

A 27-year-old housewife and insurance salesperson: "When the doctor told me I had cancer I just quit living. I laid around the house, didn't change clothes or take a bath. I must've watched TV 18 hours a day. Cried a lot. Grouched at everyone. Cursed God. Thought 'what the hell's the use.' "

The types of complaints aired above could certainly be duplicated in some form in any culture and in any historical epoch. By themselves they have no direct implications about particular forms of social expression. However, if individuals experiencing these types of tensions become involved in social networks carrying information about some potential cure, they become receptive to the literature, people, and organization that provides the mechanism to give them control over these problem areas.

Summary

The strains discussed above all involved perceptions of loss of control over valuable aspects of life. Three classes of strains were discussed, each affecting a distinct segment of the population. First, a relatively small number of deeply committed church members were involved in intellectual crosscurrents dealing with moral, theological, and organizational problems in the modern church. This group viewed the church, and indeed all of modern Christianity, as in advanced stages of defeat and decay. They were found primarily in Catholic colleges and seminaries and would eventually provide the leadership for the budding movement. These were the dreamers of a religious revival. Second, a somewhat larger group of individuals, also primarily college students in Catholic centers of learning, became disillusioned by what they saw as the failure of social criticism and activism to bring about an improved world order. Their experience in applying secular solutions to problems such as poverty, crime, racial tensions, and war left them cynical and without hope. This group overlaps somewhat with the first category of individuals but includes many who were not to become leaders but simply enthusiastic members very early during the formation of the movement. These were the dreamers of an improved world order. Finally, there were all those individuals belabored by problems of health and personal relationships for which there appeared little or no relief. These people would eventually comprise the bulk of the membership of the new movement. Although excited by notions of a widespread Christian revival and of an improved world order, their primary concern was relief from personal problems which rendered them powerless in a hostile world. Without this group there could be no successful movement.

4

The Search for Solutions
and the Path to the CCR

In chapter 2 we noted that various lines of research suggest that people will act in a helpless or apathetic manner if events lead them to believe that there is little connection between their behavior and subsequent outcome. This can be described as a condition of inefficiency created by prevailing definitions of reality. The belief is the determining factor, not the objective conditions of existence. Conversely, if people believe they can control the results of their behavior to some significant degree, they will act with reference to that belief, often at great odds created by the objective conditions of their existence. This is a state of felt efficacy, or hope.

The goal of this chapter is to highlight events that occurred in the lives of those mentioned in previous chapters which gave them hope and led to the exploration of alternatives to existing conditions. Specific events were interpreted as evidence that Christianity in general, and the Roman Catholic Church in particular, could be rescued from the secular-scientific dragon which seemed to be devouring all other competing ideologies. More importantly, some of these events appeared to demonstrate that sacred means existed for controlling the personal and collective world in ways superior to available secular means. In one sense this is the real beginning of an identifiable movement, the establishment of behaviors which were capable of creating feelings of heightened efficacy and which then led to shared, and eventually repeated, ritualistic acts.

Generating Alternative Perspectives I:
The Cursillo Movement

In explicating the factors that promoted perceptions of efficacy, we must begin with the men who eventually became recognized as the leaders of the CCR. It is this cadre of believers, originally introduced to each other as students at Notre Dame University, who searched long and diligently for mechanisms which would allow them to commit others to the task of renewing what they perceived as a weakened and dying church. It would be a serious mistake to view this movement as a product of completely fortuitous events. In much the same way that a General Motors or an A.T. & T. corporation forms and grows, the CCR is the result of sound decisions made at crucial junctures by a small group of people.

Among several individuals who were instrumental in providing form for the early CCR, Steve Clark and Ralph Martin had a disproportionate impact on this process. Clark, a former graduate student in philosophy and a man described as brilliant by those who know him, is a quiet, somewhat self-effacing individual (at least in public) who converted to Catholicism as a young adult. Martin, on the other hand, is a man of somewhat stiking presence and impressive oratorical skils who had been raised in the Roman Catholic tradition, abandoned it, and later returned to it after much soul searching and conflict. One informant, a cleric who was involved in some of those earliest days at Notre Dame, depicted Clark as the primary idea person and organizer of the movement and Martin as a public relations expert. Others thought that those character-izations failed to do justice to Martin's substantial intellectual input into the movement. However, there was unanimous agreement that Clark was the principal seed that germinated and guided the growth of the CCR.

In chapter 1 we referred to Clark as the movement's theoretician and master designer. We reached this conclusion after reading much of the movement's literature, including Clark's own writings; after frequent discussions with key informants who had intimate knowledge of events at Notre Dame and later at East Lansing, Michigan, and Ann Arbor, Michigan; and after piecing together materials written in newsletters and unpublished documents. For example, on those occasions when the movement needs to be publicly defended against detractors, Clark is the person who answers the charges. Our subsequent remarks will focus on Clark but the reader must keep in mind that Martin, and several others, were integrally involved in the events to be described.

While doing graduate work in philosophy at Notre Dame, Clark's im-pressions that Christianity was fighting a losing battle with secular hu-manism were reinforced by the relative absence of religious commitment exhibited by the bulk of the students at this ostensibly religious institu-tion. It was there that Clark began his quest to save the church. How-ever, ideas are some result of an individual's experience. As capable and far-sighted as Clark may be, it is also clear that several things shaped his thinking. One was his experiences in the Cursillo movement. In our view the Cursillo movement was a training experience in commitment techniques for the men who eventually shaped the CCR. In this sense the Cursillo movement was a stage in the development of the much more successful CCR. Fichter (1975) also sees a tie between the Cursillo movement and the CCR, but expresses surprise that more of his sample of group leaders were not Cursillo participants. This surprise can only be the result of not seeing the actual impact on the key leadership, who almost unanimously experienced the Cursillo. All social forms stable enough to be recognized as a movement go through various trial and error stages until mechanisms are found which are capable of attracting and committing individuals to patterned behavior for long enough periods of time to be recognized as a social form by observers.

The Cursillo movement reportedly began in Majorca in 1949 and found its way to the Spanish-speaking peoples of the southwestern United States around 1958. From there it spread throughout the United States (Trepanier, 1968). The Cursillo's cofounder, Bishop Juan Hervas (Duvan, 1962), has defined it as "an instrument of Christian renovation in which the most modern pedagogic, religious, sociological and psychological methods are brought into harmonious fusion with the traditional doctrine of the Church."

Two aspects of that definition are worthy of note. First, the Cursillo is defined as an instrument of renovation. Many articles discussing it specifically mention renewal. The primary goal of the Cursillo and of the CCR is identical: renewal of the church and Christianity through the spiritual renewal of individuals. Second, the Cursillo employs social science knowledge about human behavior to lead people to a recommitment to sacred values. This results in an undisguised manipulative aspect of the Cursillo which has brought much vociferous criticism. It is this particular characteristic of the Cursillo that we will focus on, since the general techniques of social control found effective in the Cursillo were later adopted in some form in the CCR.

First, the Cursillo leaders obviously recognized that if one wishes to build a stable organization that will appeal to others, then one recruits members of a relatively high economic status, members with demonstrated leadership characteristics, and members who are above serious reproach in their behavior. *The Cursillo Leaders Manual* tells us that only those of "recognized human capability, of strong and balanced personality, and of influence in their areas" (here it specifies a number of high-prestige occupations) should be selected (p. 201). Those of lesser occupational prestige ("manual laborers, workers, clerks and office workers") must display qualities of leadership recognized and legitimated by others (p. 201). Above all, "be extremely careful not to admit those who because of psychological and psychopathic conditions might harm the intense spiritual and emotional activity that is developing in the Cursillo" (p. 201). There is little ambiguity in these instructions: to optimize the possibility of success, select your participants carefully. There appears to be little opportunity in the Cursillo for those to whom religion is traditionally supposed to appeal: the downtrodden, the oppressed, the destitute, and those with substantial physical and psychic problems. To have any realistic possibility of rescuing Christianity, one begins with a cadre of influential, impeccable, and loyal models who have the ability to attract and commit others.

Second, leadership is carefully chosen among clerics and lay persons who have gone through the Cursillo experience and have unambiguously demonstrated their allegiance to its goals and methods. Both Steve Clark and Ralph Martin rose to positions of considerable influence in the national Cursillo organization. Indeed, as we shall see, Clark became one of the Cursillo's most outspoken defenders.

A Cursillo is essentially an intensive weekend experience involving lectures, carefully controlled individual and group participation, and covert surveillance designed to provide information useful in manipulating participants. In addition, supportive group structures are organized to help maintain the participants' new-found commitment beyond the single weekend experience.

Over the three-day period of the Cursillo, a series of talks, called "rollos," are given. The term "rollo" is Spanish for "roller," or talks that are basically designed to role-over, or overwhelm, the listener. These talks are orchestrated into a series of three themes, which have been selected for their maximal psychological impact. The first theme, or phase, is designed to be low-key with very little direct pressure. The goal at this stage is to attempt to reduce any resistance that may exist due to the participant's anxiety that someone is out to convert him or her. The second theme involves the generation of anxiety and self-doubt. At this stage the talks stress that whatever the Cursillista was prior to the Cursillo, he or she was woefully inadequate as a Christian. This is the beginning of the effort to "form" the Cursillista ("not to be formed is to be deformed," p. 142). Anxiety is also aroused by emphasizing the difficulty one will have living a Christian life once out of the Cursillo milieu. Secular society is depicted as a hostile environment; and it is at this point that the necessity for forming post-Cursillo support groups is presented to participants. The final theme concerns complete commitment to the Cursillo's goals, and emphasis is placed on activity which dramatizes and sustains that commitment.

The pattern of delivery of the rollos is clearly meant to maximize their impact on the listener by using well-known social psychological techniques of message presentation. The listener is initially disarmed by avoiding any semblance of high pressure techniques. The listener is then made anxious, and self-doubt engendered, so that group support and definitions of reality become more important. Finally, the Cursillo way is presented as the way to cure self-doubt and anxiety, and as a method to help ensure a more secure and controlled future.

This explicit orchestration of desired definitions of reality pervades the Cursillo experience. For example, one interesting aspect of the Cursillo leadership is the individual termed an "auxiliary." This auxilliary is an established Cursillo leader who is assigned to each small group during a Cursillo session but who passes as an ordinary participant. In other words, the auxiliary is a group plant who is not identified as a leader until the end of the Cursillo weekend. It is the role of the auxiliary to help ensure that things keep moving according to plan with a minimum of conflict and confusion. The auxiliary reinforces desired responses from participants by providing encouragement when "correct" responses are given. He looks for possible trouble and provides information on those participants who may require extra attention and counseling. He also attempts to dampen conflict and criticism, which could disrupt the sequence of events and weaken the definition of reality being orchestrated by the leaders.

Written records are kept on each participant so that the spiritual director will have sufficient data "to be able to form the most complete idea possible of their [participants] psychological and moral makeup" (p. 249). For example, after the Cursillistas have gone to bed, all the leaders meet privately to discuss the participants and their individual progress. During these meetings, plans are designed to provide subtle pressure on individuals who do not appear to be making satisfactory progress. As in CCR leadership meetings, Cursillo leadership meetings begin with an invocation to the Holy Spirit for proper guidance and inspiration.

Some critics (see Wills, 1965) of the Cursillo have suggested that fatigue is systematically induced through the mechanism of long talks, late hours, and early risings. Fatigue is very useful in cooling opposition and making the individual more receptive to communications that might ordinarily be resisted.

The precision and explicitness of the manipulative side of the Cursillo is clearly outlined in the following statements from the *Leaders Manual:*

The psychology of the cursillistas on this third day is usually as follows:

In order to respond to the psychological situation, to channel it effectively and dissipate sterile pessimism, instilling in the new soldier high combat morale, the leaders must make an orderly arrangement of the acts of this third day.

Many times during the day the "slogan"—"all is provided for"—will be repeated to the cursillistas in compliance with the logical and chronological development of the theme being presented to them (pp. 145–146).

The closing ceremony usually involves intense emotionality and has some of the elements characterizing revival meetings. There is a good deal of testimony from veteran Cursillistas. This testimony often revolves around the security which the Cursillo has brought to the individual's life and other positive results of embracing the Cursillo way. It is common to find participants weeping in response to the emotions generated by this impressive ceremony.

The parallel between this orchestrated experience and the phenomenon labeled "brainwashing" has been suggested by some of the Cursillo's critics (see Coutourier, 1964). The term "brainwashing" was coined in the mid 1950s by a journalist in order to depict the resocialization process used by the North Koreans and the Chinese communists to elicit false confessions from American prisoners of war. The process involved severe physical deprivations, completely controlled communications, and incessant assaults on the individual's self-esteem (Schein, 1961; Hunter, 1951; Lifton, 1961). However, while there may be parallels between the structure of the Cursillo and brainwashing, the differences are substantial. The Cursillo does not involve the individual for an extended period—it is ludicrous to suggest that an unwitting individual can be brainwashed in three days; it does not involve intense physical and psychological coercion—Cursillo participants are not shackled, forced to eat out of troughs like pigs, nor are their bodily functions handled like an infant's; and it does not go to extremes to strip the individual of past self-referents. Unfortunately, the term "brainwashing" has become a handy acronym that can be used to attack those with whom we disagree. For example, we could show analogies between brainwashing and certain facets of the modern feminist movement, the experience of the middle class child in modern American society, or the experience of university students anywhere. In other words, if I am trying to influence someone to my way of thinking, that is termed "education." If you are trying to influence someone to your way of thinking, a way I disapprove of, that will be termed "brainwashing."

Most of the effects of intense brainwashing were very short-lived once the person was removed from the actual controlled environment, while the effects of the Cursillo appear to last well beyond the actual Cursillo experience. This would seem to indicate that the Cursillo message is falling on receptive ears. Perceived volition is extremely important in sustaining a newly adopted perspective (see chapter 2).

While we disagree that the Cursillo methods resemble brainwashing, these methods obviously involve known techniques of social influence, including attacks on old identities, purposely engendered anxiety, promises of a fuller and more secure future, public testimony and public surveillance, tight group control under the guidance of a surreptitious "plant," group control through criticism and comment about the individual's own written and art work, and, to help ensure post-Cursillo commitment, the assignment of Cursillistas to groups designed to continue monitoring and sanctioning the inductee's behavior after the return home.

The post-Cursillo groups are formed on the basis of common interests indicated in information provided at the start of the Cursillo. Groups formed on the basis of common interests are more likely to survive and be cohesive. Especially fervent Cursillistas were often assigned to more than one group in order to help maintain desired levels of commitment. This is also an effective means of ensuring that a core group of leaders are in a position to control policy through interlocking memberships.

The post-Cursillo groups have weekly meetings during which the Cursillistas's progress is checked and appropriately sanctioned. These meetings also involve a considerable emphasis on personal testimonies indicating "apostolic successes" and "apostolic failures," plus the discussion of those moments when the individuals felt closest to Christ. Noncompliance with assigned obligations is met with varying degrees of negative sanctions leveled by the group.

As indicated throughout this discussion of the Cursillo, many critics have leveled charges of purposive manipulation at Cursillo leaders. Steven Clark's reply (1965) to these critics is a succinct statement of his philosophy of human learning and decision making:

> In order to evaluate the negative opinion of the Cursillo, something must be brought out that is simply overlooked . . . the context in which the Cursillo uses "psychological means." This context includes both the situation of the candidates for the Cursillo and the nature of Christianity. Both articles (here Clark is referring to critical articles) assume that the men who come to the Cursillo are free men in respect to their Christianity. They assume that they are highly rational, reflective individuals who have carefully thought out their attitudes to life and to Christianity, and that all is needed is a clear, attractive presentation of Christianity which can be offered for their consideration.
>
> This is simply a myth. the men who come to the Cursillo are in large part the product of their environment. They live daily solidly cemented into an

> environment which is indifferent to Christ and indifferent to many Chris-
> tian values. And they have been *conditioned* by their environment [em-
> phasis added] . . . In evaluating the Cursillo, it is important to realize
> both that the chief obstacle to a fuller Christian life is a man's enslave-
> ment to a secular environment and that full Christianity involves being
> part of a Christian community . . . therefore, to describe what the Cursillo
> is doing as subjecting a man to the pressure of the group is not quite
> accurate, because it implies that he was originally free of such pressure
> and that a man can be a Christian without any group pressure (that is,
> without being part of any group). The strategy of the Cursillo is to take a
> man out of a situation in which the group pressure is strongly secular and
> put him in a situation in which the group pressure is Christian and in
> which he can experience a true Christian community.

In this statement Clark recognizes the importance of the social environment, even to the point of using the term "conditioned" to refer to
people's adherence to secular values. Consequently, Clark sees no wrong
in systematically influencing people, as long as the ends justify the
means. Indeed "manipulation" for Christ is deemed desirable. Clark
obviously recognizes the importance of group support and surveillance in
maintaining the individual's "proper" definition of the situation. Clark
also realizes the importance of emotional involvement in cementing
commitment to group goals. This explicit structuring of the social environment to manipulate people in ways commensurate with group goals
is something that apparently has characterized Clark's entire approach
to problems of Christian renewal. It is evident in the Cursillo Movement
and in the Antioch Weekends (retreats and talks aimed at the "special
psychology" of the college student), and will become evident as we further discuss the development of the CCR.

Our purpose in making this point is not to cast Clark in the role of
some schemeing Machiavellian nor to question his assumptions about
human learning and motivation. As social scientists, we tend to agree
with his basic assumptions; and certainly Clark is no more Machiavellian
than anyone who attempts to influence others in ways defined as desirable, such as parents, teachers, preachers, business leaders, or adver-
tisers. The point is that Clark has a good fundamental understanding of
the social nature of the human animal and uses this understanding to
help build a body of believers bent on preserving Christianity. Subsequent events that occurred on the road to the contemporary CCR become
much more intelligible in this light, and can be viewed as a pattern
rather than a series of isolated incidences.

In the Cursillo we saw the emphasis on the Holy Spirit, the uses of
small group pressures, emotionality, public testimony, and carefully orchestrated definitions of reality. All of these elements will eventually be

found in the CCR. They will be incorporated by the same men who used them in the Cursillo. However, the Cursillo is not an optimal method to promote a set of values. It reaches a much too limited segment of the population and lacks means to attract large numbers of people. It is also too ephemeral an experience to ensure individual commitment. Most importantly, the mechanisms it uses to increase participants' feelings of efficacy are too limited to provide that level of involvement necessary to build a successful movement.

So, even though there existed a cadre of committed, intelligent men and women, well versed in methods of constructing reality for others, two elements remained before an entirely successful movement could emerge. Something had to happen which would dislodge a substantial number of people, especially Catholics, from the forces shaping their existing definitions of reality; in addition, something dramatic had to occur which would give these dislodged people greater feelings of efficacy in an environment perceived as increasingly hostile.

Generating Alternative Perspectives II: Vatican II

The first of these events was the second Vatican Council in 1963 and its unanticipated aftermath. As previously discussed, Vatican II was an attempt by the church to respond to developments in modern science, philosophy, and political realities, which undermined the authority of a number of church practices and ideological stances. The importance of the Vatican II documents was that they promoted a popular interpretation of greater philosophical liberalism on the part of the church and, at least for a time, seemed to approve of limited liturgical experimentation among the laity. Equally important was the relative absence of explicit guidelines designed to implement the Vatican II pronouncements. This ambiguity ensured grass roots experimentation and attempts to recast religious life in ways made more viable by the Vatican II documents.

Most of the major themes of Vatican II were to become the major emphases of the CCR. For example, the opening message of the Council stressed self-renewal, with guidance from the Holy Spirit, so that the individual could be more authentically Christian. Indeed, throughout the documents of Vatican II the Holy Spirit is continually mentioned in the context of renewing and rejuvenating the church. Even more dramatically, Pope John XXIII had prayed that Vatican II might be a "New Pentecost." In adopting the position that the CCR is a direct result of the workings of the Holy Spirit, its leadership could eventually claim that the movement is a response to the mandates of Vatican II. In fact, the movement's legitimacy can be argued from the perspective that the Holy Spirit inspired the Second Vatican Council, and then was responsible for the inception of the CCR, which is to be the mechanism for realizing Vatican II's objectives. The entire process can be viewed as a result of divine inspiration and planning. This is the position that is implied in the writings emanating from the movement and its supporters.

The entire thrust of Vatican II's treatment of authority relations also finds a concrete expression in the authority structure within the CCR. The document entitled "Lumen Gentium" depicted authority in terms of service rather than of domination. It was designed to democratize the church. Later sections continue this emphasis by stressing the human and social nature of the church while downplaying any attention to the institutional and the hierarchical.

While much is often made of Vatican II's doctrine of collegiality, which appeared to give bishops greater decision making power, more pertinent to the CCR are the writings concerning the role of the layman in the church power structure. Specifically, the article on deacons is of momentous import.

> The diaconate can in the future be restored as a proper and permanent rank of the hierarchy. It pertains to the competent territorial bodies of bishops, of one kind or another, to decide, with the approval of the Supreme Pontiff, whether and where it is opportune for such deacons to be appointed for the care of souls. With the consent of the Roman Pontiff, the diaconate will be available to be conferred upon men of more mature age, even upon those living in the married state. It may also be conferred upon suitable young men. For them, however, the law of celibacy must remain intact (Abbott, 1966:56).

Clearly Vatican II was not simply paying lip service to the notion of increased lay participation in church affairs. It restored a practice which had the potential of ensuring official lay participation in the church hierarchy. The CCR was to exemplify this democratization thrust with a vengeance. Even though clerics often play a significant and at times dominant role in prayer groups, communities, and regional, national, and international offices of the CCR, CCR leadership has attempted to keep clerical participation at the membership level. In recent years participation by clerics has mushroomed. The significance of this will be discussed in subsequent sections. It is especially prominent in the covenanted communities patterned after Clark and Martin's former community, the Word of God community in Ann Arbor, Michigan. During an interview with Martin in 1973, we inquired whether this group encouraged clerical participation. He made it very clear that, while clerics were certainly welcome as participants, any evidence of their unearned ascension to power in the prayer group or the community was discouraged. A growing number of CCR laymen have been pursuing the diaconate in recent years. Kevin Ranaghan, an early and influential CCR leader, was one of the first to be made a deacon. The CCR clearly views itself as a concrete expression of Vatican II's emphasis on lay leadership.

At least as important as the items mentioned above is Vatican II's explicit treatment of the charismatic gifts.

> It is not only through the sacraments and Church ministries that the same Holy Spirit sanctifies and leads the People of God and enriches it with virtues. Allotting His gifts "to everyone according as he will" (1 Corinthians 12:11), He distributes special graces among the faithful of every rank . . . These Charismatic gifts, whether they be the most outstanding or the more simple and widely diffused, are to be received with Thanksgiving and consolation for they are exceedingly suitable and useful for the needs of the Church (Abbott, 1966:10).

In line with the overall democratic trend of Vatican II's documents, this statement makes it clear that the rituals of the church are not the sole source of grace. At times God works directly through his people without the church as intermediary. This statement, and others of similar import (for example, the document on laity, p. 492), opened the door to Catholics engaging in religious activities that in the past would have been regarded with both suspicion and distaste. However, Vatican II also sounded a cautionary note:

> Still, extraordinary gifts are not to be rashly sought after nor are the fruits of apostolic labor to be presumptuously expected from them. In any case, judgment as to their genuineness and proper use belongs to those who preside over the Church, and to whose special competence it belongs (Abbott, 1966:30).

So, in the final analysis, the church is still the final arbiter of all religious activity. Vatican II may have legitimated activities such as those found in the CCR, but it still reserves the right to judge their propriety.

In conjunction with the explicit treatment of charisms in the everyday life of the practicing Christian is the strong treatment of the biblical nature of Christianity—at least strong when compared to the past. In sharp contrast to the intellectual approach to the Bible that characterized post-Reformation Catholicism, Vatican II treated the Bible as a living document that is a means to unite a human being and God. The "Dogmatic Constitution on Divine Revelation" tells us that "The important point is here made that biblical faith is far more than an intellectual assent to propositions. It is a loyal adherence to a personal God" (Abbott, 1966:108). Here again is a clarion call for a personalized Christianity,

Christ as experienced by the believer, or the community of believers, and not simply as mediated by the church.

Another major thrust of Vatican II that is mirrored in the CCR is the stress on ecumenicity, the unity of all believers. Clearly recognizing the defeatist aspects of ruptured Christianity, Vatican II attempts to draw an umbrella of union over all Christians. This umbrella is stretched to include Jews, Moslems, and even various nonbelievers who "sincerely follow the lights God gives them." From a perspective which formerly stressed the return of the stray sheep to the fold, Vatican II creates an image of all "people of God" moving together toward Christ.

This focus on Christian unity, along with a relative deemphasis of doctrinal differences, added to the general themes developed throughout the Vatican II documents: Christian unity and good example in the face of an increasingly hostile secular world, greater participation and freedom of choice, and an apparent relaxation of long-standing defensiveness against those who held less than absolute allegiance to the Pope. As with the themes discussed previously, the CCR was to create an environment in which the ecumenical thrust of Vatican II could be given concrete expression. In the prayer groups and communities that we sampled, approximately 20 percent of the participants are Protestants. These are almost exclusively members of main line Protestant bodies. There is virtually a complete absence of members of pentecostal churches, although noted leaders from the pentecostal churches do participate in national and regional conventions organized by the CCR. The actual distribution of Protestants in prayer groups and communities varies from many groups who have none to those like the Ann Arbor community, which has approximately 50 percent Protestant membership. Furthermore, the ecumenical theme is one which pervades the pages of *New Covenant*, the major document of the CCR and largely the work of the Ann Arbor group.

Finally, there is a strong theme of community in the documents of Vatican II. For example, the document on religious freedom states:

> Because love ever seeks to communicate, back of religious freedom there is found a commitment to community. The notion that "religion is a purely private matter" has no place in a Christian document. To define religious freedom in purely subjective and individualistic terms is to misconceive its essential nature and to build in sand. The true end of freedom is the growth of love and service to the neighbor (Abbott, 1966:697).

The document on the laity also emphasized the group apostolate because "man is naturally social" and "where two or three are gathered together for my sake, there am I in the midst of them" (Matthew 18:20). "The

Church in the Modern World" unambiguously portrays the individual as an outcome of his or her social relations. To say that community is an emphasis in the CCR would be an understatement. Steve Clark views tight, cohesive Christian communities as the only salvation for Christianity in an increasingly secular world. In recent months CCR leadership has been probing the possibility of a federation of prayer communities. More will be said of this development in chapters 6 and 7.

Both the Cursillo movement and Vatican II were concerned with renovating or renewing the church through the renewal of individuals. The Cursillo movement gave Clark and other eventual leaders of the CCR some practical training in techniques of committing individuals to predefined lines of action. Vatican II presented a plan for a renewal that coincided with Clark's ideas concerning the proper path to renewal. Clark and the others at Notre Dame were keenly aware of the Vatican II pronouncements.

At least as important as the specific themes developed by Vatican II was its reluctance to develop an explicit program that would move toward the stated goals. The goals were stated in rather abstract terms with a corresponding absence of directives designed to guide the behavior of informed, interested Roman Catholics. This situation encouraged exploration and the perception of alternatives. University communities in particular saw a rash of liturgical experimentation following on the heels of Vatican II. The first author of this monograph took part in prayer meetings (noncharismatic), home Masses, and other flights into religious freedom manifested by young, educated Catholics in the aftermath of Vatican II. Reports from friends at other campuses indicated the widespread nature of this experimentation. Again it must be stressed that this experimentation did not involve anything like a majority of Roman Catholics at these institutions of higher learning. These were primarily a handful of devoted, educated, well-informed young people. But the intensity and dedication of these students certainly matched that of their activist colleagues who were marching in the streets. In fact many of these "renewing" Catholics were also social activists of varying degrees of militancy. This was true of Steve Clark and others involved in beginnings of the CCR. At the Sixth National Cursillo Conference, in which Clark played a leadership role, a great deal of activity involved a public commitment to antiracist and antiwar positions and other popular liberal causes of the day. These young people now had some useful techniques, a program, and increased enthusiasm, which could be channeled into a full-fledged movement. All the elements for a successful movement were present except one: there was still an absence of techniques which would allow this nucleus to commit others who were perhaps less intense in their desire to save Christianity. They still did not have a means of committing a wider membership.

Generating Alternative Perspectives III: The "Miracles"

During the period of emerging prayer groups and intense prayer that was stimulated by the Second Vatican Council, two books were read by the group at Notre Dame which were instrumental in leading to the final elements necessary for the development of a movement. One book, *The Cross and the Switchblade* (Wilkerson, 1964), was written by an Assembly of God minister and chronicles the events which led him from a small Pennsylvania community to the teenage gangland of New York City. Several miraculous events are detailed by Wilkerson. First, the motivation which led him to travel to New York in a blind groping to help teenage gangs is attributed to some external source, other than the self. He speaks of thoughts coming into his head "as though it had come into me from somewhere else," of thoughts being "completely independent" of his own volition (p. 7), and of seeking and receiving signs from God. The whole series of events is viewed as a leading from the Holy Spirit. At one point he has a friend open the Bible in a search for some legitimation for his undertaking, and the friend comes up with an encouraging passage from the 126th Psalm (p. 14).

Later Wilkerson is traveling through New York City, whose geography he does not know, and recieves an interior message to stop suddenly. This stop puts him in contact with members of the gang that he is interested in. Later he accidentally parks his car right in front of the house of a youth he is searching for, even though he has no notion of where the youth lives. The rest of the book concerns his successes and failures in attempting to turn the gang youths toward a Christian life style. The gang leader even is cured of a lifelong speech problem and is completely converted to Wilkerson's Christianity. Wilkerson refers to these events as "undeniable miracles" (p. 33). Assuming the veracity of his story, these events are indeed difficult to account for through conventional wisdom. The events are highly improbable, and their rate of occurrence appears to refute the random coincidence type of explanation. Whatever their cause, this was exactly the type of information the would-be world builders at Notre Dame were looking for: apparently incontrovertible evidence that God was directly intervening in the lives of modern man. To idealistic young men who were witnessing the final throes of a social activist attempt to save the world, this was indeed heady wine. Now they had "evidence" that spiritual means existed to save the world, and these spiritual means seemed to promise a power far in excess of that power they had experienced in social activism. Furthermore, the Holy Spirit they had been praying to so intensely was for them the genesis of Wilkerson's unusual odyssey. This was a "sign" that revitalized the seekers at Notre Dame.

The second key book, John Sherrill's *They Speak with Other Tongues* (1964), describes the author's discovery of personalized, emotional Christianity. After a second cancer operation, Sherrill experienced what appears to be the presence of Christ in his hospital room. A subsequent meeting with Harold Bredesen, a noted pentecostal, introduced Sherrill to the tongue speaking phenomenon and baptism in the spirit. Sherrill then researched tongue speaking both historically and by collecting reports of other people's experiences. He concluded that tongue speaking is biblically valid, a gift given by the Holy Spirit which has miraculous properties and is a superior method of totally committing Christians to their religion. Sherrill eventually spoke in tongues and experienced the overwhelming joy that others have reported after their initial ventures into glossolalia. He ends his chronicle with the suggestion that pentecostalism has the potential to unite and recommit all Christians.

While Wilkerson's book provided a general uplift to the Notre Dame seekers by describing events that could be interpreted as modern miracles, Sherrill's points to a specific method that has the ability to provide individuals with a new sense of wonder in and allegiance to a diffuse Christianity.[1] All the seekers had to do now was to find someone who could teach them tongue speaking and could baptize in the spirit. Filled with hope and mounting expectation, they continue to pray and to search. In February, 1967, a contingency from Notre Dame went to Duquesne University (Clark and Martin were not among them) for a religious retreat. Two of this contingency specifically sought out a pentecostal service so that they might witness tongue speaking and baptism in the spirit. Their experience is best described by their own words: "A little group of Protestants have shown us what it really means to be Catholics. And more than that, the Spirit of God is mightily at work here." These two went back to the Dusquesne retreat, where the participants were already in an intense, receptive state, and tongue speaking and baptism in the spirit were experienced by those expectant Catholics. The feelings of joy and wonder were such that this core of people began communicating with friends of similar persuasion, among them Clark and Martin, who soon journeyed to Pittsburgh and also experienced baptism in the spirit and tongue speaking.

---

[1]The word "diffuse" is carefully chosen here because one outstanding facet of neopentecostalism is the absence of any serious doctrinal considerations. The goal, often stated, is to build a Christian community similar to those that reportedly characterized the earliest days of Christianity.

The intensity and enthusiasm generated by these novel experiences were enough to convince Clark and Martin that they now had the mechanism needed to attract a wider following and to commit people at a distance. These experiences were relayed from university community to university community across the country through sociometric channels of close friends who were already involved in post-Vatican II intense religious seeking. The CCR was now on its way to becoming a successful social movement. Clark and Martin, and others in the early Notre Dame group of seekers, were to guide it and provide the frame which would determine the shape the movement was eventually to take. However, to completely understand why baptism in the spirit and the other "gifts" are such a powerful mechanism of commitment, a more detailed social psychological analysis of their impact is required. That is the subject of the next chapter.

Summary

In one sense, the actual beginning of the CCR involved the diffusion of several types of information which gave traditional Catholics the perception that there were positive things they could do to stem the tide of secularism.

The involvement of eventual CCR leaders in the Cursillo movement provided them with experience in organizing and running intensive small group sessions which were designed to enhance and reinstate religious commitment. The effectiveness of these managed experiences were dramatic enough to convince eventual CCR leaders of the importance of interpersonal involvement and ongoing group support. The subsequent CCR emphasis on intense social support as a necessity to maintain belief in the face of a hostile environment stemmed from the lessons of the Cursillo movement.

The upheaval engendered by Vatican II also made the CCR possible. The various Vatican II documents were interpreted as an affirmation of the liberal elements in the church. The doors now seemed open to liturgical experimentation and more individualized expressions of Christianity. Greater power was to be exercised by the laity.

Specific themes emanating from the Vatican II documents and subsequent attempts to put these themes into practice also helped create a climate in which the CCR could emerge. Student groups at a number of Catholic colleges and universities began putting these themes into practice. This network of small groups of experimenting Catholics who were seeking a rebirth of Biblical Christianity provided the foundations for an emerging social movement. What was needed to launch this new vessel was some powerful affirmation that their seeking was divinely supported. This affirmation was to come through contact with Protestant pentecostals.

The emerging leadership of the CCR read books which told of miracles experienced by some Protestant pentecostals. Encouraged by this news of the Holy Spirit at work in modern society, some Catholic college students sought out noted Protestant pentecostals and, given their teaching and example, experienced baptism in the spirit. This core group was the nucleus of the CCR. The movement had begun.

5
Commitment and Social Control: The Gifts of the Spirit

> To this day, many Christians give little evidence that their lives are any different from the lives of non-Christians. Certainly, this is no testimony to the saintliness of non-believers; rather it is a tragic reflection on the powerlessness in the lives of many believers (Basham, 1977).

Every organization not having an inducement and reward system that is primarily economic must have activities which lead participants to a sense of greater self-efficacy as a result of belonging and participation. Secret ceremonies, concrete symbols indicating achievement, special languages, intense interpersonal support, frequent reminders of past successes, recollection of how far the group has come since its humble beginnings, and ritualistic behavior involving an aura of mystery give the individual an enhanced sense of worth and efficacy. The gifts of the spirit serve this function most admirably, and are instruments in establishing social control over individuals.

Social Control and the Interface of Commitment

It is a sociological truism that all organizations exert control to ensure the achievement of valued goals. Etzioni (1961) offers a useful typology of control mechanisms and the kind of member involvement each type of control engenders. Control can be exercised through coercion or the use of pure power, such as prisons. This type of control generates alienation in its participants. Control can also be exercised through the use of economic inducements, as in blue and white collar industries, and results in a mode of involvement Etzioni terms "calculative." In other words, people contribute resources to the organization because of anticipated monetary rewards. Finally, control can take the form of voluntary allegiance to organizational norms. Etzioni suggests that this type of involvement is moral, as with churches and ideological movements.

While it is true that Etzioni's typology usefully illuminates somewhat distinctive characteristics of organizations, it tends to leave some important questions of social control unanswered, although, in fairness to Etzioni, his typology was quite adequate given the level of analysis his work was directed toward. Etzioni's work, like a great deal of work in sociology, reflects a fundamental ambivalence: the vacillation between voluntaristic and deterministic models of man. An examination of Etzioni's three kinds of power leads the reader to conclude that the normative type is significantly different from the other two types, since it is primarily voluntary. That is, the person chooses to engage in the behavior with a minimum of external inducements.

We have decided to be less ambivalent and adopt a position closer to B.F. Skinner's and Steve Clark's avowedly deterministic one. In chapter 3 we suggested that perspectives (norms, definitions of situations, and supporting activities) are probably conditioned by (a) prior learning, which encourages appreciation and acceptance of some perspectives but anxiety with or rejection of others; (b) socioenvironmental conditions of conflict and strain, especially when coupled with ambiguity which favors perspectives promising rather immediate feelings of efficacy; (c) contact with groups championing a given viewpoint in the context of a powerful reward structure; and (d) the neophyte's perception that a novel perspective has been freely chosen. In other words, Etzioni's "normative" organizations with their "moral" involvement are those which the individual is channeled into by personal and social factors, and which are structured in such a way that the individual perceives a personal rather than a situational or external cause. The gifts of the spirit, and the social context of their manifestation, offer dramatic perceptions of heightened efficacy in a group setting providing written, verbal, and behavioral models in a joyful and loving manner. Although reception of the gifts is strongly encouraged, it is not pushed or forced, and is thus perceived as a voluntary act. Acts perceived as voluntary increase commitment. Where more high powered evangelistic techniques have been used, thereby promoting an external attribution of cause, dissatisfaction and group dissolution have been the result. The rise and fall of the True House community at Notre Dame will eventually be discussed in this context.

There are many gifts referred to in the Bible, particularly in Paul's letters to the Corinthians (see chapters 12–14 of First Corinthians). In these messages Paul enumerates the following gifts of the spirit: wisdom, knowledge, healing, miraculous powers, prophecy, distinguishing good and evil spirits, tongues and the interpretation of tongues, and others. Although each of these gifts find mention in the pages of *New Covenant* and during prayer meetings, it is clear that the most dramatic and most often considered are the gifts of tongue speaking and interpretation, prophecy, and healing. In addition there is a lesser but obvious concern with the gift of spiritual discernment. We shall discuss each of these gifts in the context of what they contribute to individual commitment, group cohesion, and social control.

Tongue Speaking and Interpretation

In discussing the importance of tongue speaking in the CCR movement, we must immediately register a caveat. While tongue speaking is a dominant characteristic of the CCR, there are those who do not speak in tongues (17 percent of our sample), and nothing we observed suggests that nonspeakers are "second class" citizens. In a number of meetings we attended there was no tongue speaking at all. However, the gifts in general, and tongues in particular, are stressed as an invaluable armor in the battle with Satan, self, and the world (see Basham, 1977; Williams, 1978). One contributer to *New Covenant* goes as far as to suggest that "those in a body who don't receive the gift of tongues suffer as a result" (Forrest, 1974). In addition, as was true of the pentecostal pioneers, manifestations of tongues appears to be the primary way that group members judge whether a neophyte has been baptized in the Holy Spirit.

Speaking in tongues is not an everyday normal linguistic activity among those who may be judged as religiously involved. Indeed, it is not per se a religious form of speech behavior, since it can occur in a purely secular context divorced from any religious significance whatsoever. It is far more widespread than most people think, and has accordingly attracted the attention of anthropologists, sociologists, psychologists, theologians, and journalists. Its presence in the church has been highly restricted and has, in the past particularly, been primarily associated with groups which have been marginal to the major expression of religion in western society. The association with marginal groups has caused some scholars to define the activity as aberrant behavior of those persons who were "nearly always the ignorant, in whom the lower brain centers and spinal ganglia are relatively strong and the rational and volitional lower brain centers of the cortex are relatively weak" (Clark, 1949:97). In short, only the stupid speak in tongues. Such an assessment was not wholly incorrect, in that those groups in which glossolalia was normative were often composed of less educated and often noneducated people. One of the reasons for the recent scholarly interest in glossolalia is that such interpretations are no longer sufficient. Sociological studies of more re-

cent vintage (see Hine, 1969; 1974; Gerlach, 1974) offer evidence which
discounts the association of glossolalia with *only* marginal religous
groups suffering from either social or psychic deprivation. Tongue speaking now occurs among main line Protestant groups, as well as among
the Catholic and Protestant pentecostals. In seeking to account for the
spread of this form of speech behavior among those groups with which
it has not been previously associated, it is necessary to reconsider former
interpretations which tended to dismiss glossolalia as a serious form of
activity among any but the highly emotional and distraught.

It is not difficult to understand why glossolalia has been considered
deviant or even weird by those who do not practice speaking in tongues.
It is probably true that today an overwhelming majority of churchgoing
types have never observed anyone speaking in tongues. When such an
occasion arises the initial reaction is, at the least, to consider such persons as different. Psychological studies of glossolalia have tended to concentrate upon looking for differences, especially pathological ones, between those who speak in tongues and those who do not. The results of
such studies are inconclusive at best. Two investigations (Vivier, unpublished, cited in Samarin, 1972; Wood, 1965) do suggest that there are
personality differences between tongue speakers and nonspeakers. Vivier
notes tendencies on the part of glossolalists toward greater emphasis
upon feelings than thought and fewer formalized thought processes.
Wood specifically postulates differences between pentecostal tongue
speakers and nonpentecostals in a southern community. Using the Rorschach test to search for differences, he reports that the pentecostals
were more likely to produce perspective, depth, and distance responses
than the nonpentecostals. However, as Wood acknowledges, even the
supporters of the Rorschach technique express disagreement over the
scoring of such responses. He also notes that such differences as he
reports may result *from* participation in pentecostal activities rather than
existing prior to such involvement. Kildahl (1972) concludes that glossolalists are "more submissive, suggestive, and dependent in the presence
of authority figures than non-tongue speakers," but overall finds no evidence for mental pathology among those who speak in tongues. Again
the submissiveness Kildahl finds may be a result of commitment to
biblical injunctions and a result of involvement in a particular religious
community rather than a determinant of tongue speaking. Cohn (1968)
and Pattison and Carey (1969) argue for a similar interpretation of
mental health among glossalists. More recently, Lovekin and Malony
(1977) report longitudinal research investigating the hypothesis that
glossolalia might enhance personality. Only one of their research results
supported that hypothesis—a significant reduction in "state anxiety"
among those who become glossolic. The entire experience with a com-

mitted religious group appeared to have the greatest effect on personality enhancement (less depression, hostility, extrinsic religiosity, fewer personal problems, and greater ego strength) quite independent of glossolalia per se. They do state that there was no evidence that those who became glossolalic were disturbed. In fact they suggest that "being more anxious, hostile, and depressed may predispose a person to being unable to become glossolalic." This would support our own observations, which suggest that those who are highly anxious and somewhat introverted appear to have a very difficult time engaging in tongue speaking.

Those who have studied glossolalia in cross-cultural settings, including non-Christian religions, also report findings which do not support the thesis that glossolalists are concentrated among the pathological. Goodman (1972), although arguing that glossolalia is an altered state of consciousness, does not view it as a pathological behavior. (In an interesting "Confession" she reports that even ethnographers are "not immune" and that she herself spoke in tongues, but only once). Similar conclusions are reached in the several studies reported in Bourguignon (1973). However, we would take issue with Goodman's thesis that glossolalia necessarily involves an altered state of consciousness. While it is true that glossolalia can be accompanied by trancelike states, especially during the initial attempts, most of the tongue speaking we observed certainly could not be so characterized. On countless occasions our middle class glossolalics have unrolled glossolic prayer with the same ease and undramatic presentation style as they would say an "Our Father." At one point a dynamic young nun, working toward her M. S. degree in science, offered to speak in tongues for us in the reserved room of the university library. Gelpi (1971) reports that he taught himself to speak in tongues by going to a chapel and quietly saying "la, la, la, la," to himself until he spoke in tongues. This intentional approach to tongue acquisition is not unique to Gelpi. There are rather obvious cultural and subcultural predispositions to trancelike states, and glossolalia in these cultures should be expected to be accompanied more often by altered states of consciousness. However, it is extremely difficult to prove the existence of altered states of consciousness. Most of the time these altered states are indexed by what is simply very emotional behavior. The judgment of an "altered state" may simply be the attribution made by an observer who reasons that such behavior could not occur without some modification of "normal" mental functioning.

Thus the early view of those who speak in tongues as being psychologically deviant, or associated primarily with groups who are socially disorganized or deviant, is not supported by empirical research. Gilmore's (1969) findings coincide with our general observations from interaction with Catholic pentecostals: "The open or non-dogmatic Pentecostal believers appear as well adjusted and interpersonally skillful as do people in general" (p. 164).

If available data suggests that glossolalists are otherwise normal and well-adjusted personality types, it should not be surprising that this speech behavior can be understood as a linguistic form which, while different from ordinary discourse in terms of its vocabulary or content, has a grammatical form that parallels the grammatical form of the speaker's common discourse. The general form of glossolalia is therefore capable of being learned as any other speech habit. What is unique from individual to individual is the content of the utterances, but even these are patterned for the individual who speaks in tongues more than once. In other words, whatever "vocabulary" the neophyte glossolalist begins with is likely to characterize subsequent expressions.

The basic ordinariness of glossolalia is the central thrust of Samarin's study. Examining the practice from a linguistic point of view, he concludes that "glossolalia is a perfectly human, perfectly normal (albeit anomalous) phenomena" (1972:35). It can be produced experimentally—that is, subjects can be taught to speak in tongues—as Pattison and Carey, Goodman, Cohn, Kildahl, and others report.

From a sociological perspective, the more interesting question may be why glossolalia has been viewed with such popular and professional wonderment and alarm. The functions of special languages has been known since antiquity. So-called expressive languages—those uttered during heightened emotional states, which express that state but have little connection between the words used and the things or acts they denote—are part of every culture. The use of foreign languages or idiosyncratic terminology to enhance the users' perception of special wisdom and power, and as control devices, are common to professions such as law, medicine, sociology, and even psychiatry. Unusual linguistic forms are commonly found in both children's and adults' special groups, and are used primarily to increase the member's perception of being special because of such membership. As will be subsequently discussed, glossolalia performs these identical functions for its practitioners.

For the pentecostals, however, speaking in tongues is something more than a perfectly human, perfectly normal act. To understand just what glossolalia means to members of the CCR, we turn to the best possible source—those who speak in tongues.

We asked our respondents if they had received the gift of tongues, and if so, what this experience meant for them. The dominant response (67 percent of those speaking in tongues) was similar to that of a 41-year-old housewife: "The ability to allow the Holy Spirit to pray through me in praise or petition when I'm at a loss for words to communicate my deepest desires."

Others echo this position by using such phrases as "when my human vocabulary is not enough," or "I can pray in a specific way when I run out of words." These constant references to God speaking through the individual in prayer designates the function of glossolalia as an aide to efficacious prayer. The Holy Spirit praying through an individual enables a higher form of prayer than that which is possible when one prays simply within the conventional idiom. Glossolalia for the Catholic pentecostal is a religious experience in the context of the larger experiential dimensions of religion so heavily emphasized in the movement. For the pentecostal believer, it is prayer above and beyond the natural language. It thus is a supernatural form of behavior and perceived as a gift of the spirit.

However, to define glossolalia as an expressive speech that is easily learned through modeling or practice or both, which the practitioner defines as a higher form of prayer, does not do justice to the functions tongue speaking serves for individuals, groups, and the CCR as a whole. A message in tongues is testimony to the active presence of God's word in our day in a manner not ordinarily given. A message in this context further strengthens the participant's belief that it is through the CCR that God is to renew the church. It adds a high note of distinctiveness to what the movement stands for and is trying to accomplish. Many religious groups may feel that they are doing the will of God, but here is evidence of a different sort that God is in a special way speaking through those who have received the gift of tongues. Tongues in this context become a reinforcement for the belief that the individual has something special to offer his or her less fortunate brothers and sisters, an excellent justification for expecting the church to be renewed within the framework offered by the CCR.

Social theoreticians and practitioners have recognized that under certain circumstances, personal humiliation and suffering can be very important in increasing an individual's commitment to the group. Fraternities and sororities, elite military units, secret societies, and elite private and community organizations sometimes have initiation ceremonies designed to humiliate and place the initiate under a great deal of physical and psychic strain. Besides the group-induced personal suffering, two other elements are viewed as necessary to help ensure that the outcome is increased individual commitment to the group: the humiliation and suffering must be public, and the initiate must perceive that he or she has voluntarily taken on the burdens of the activity. If the behavior is not voluntarily adopted, the individual simply attributes his or her misery to some external agent, and there is no need for a self-justifying or other type of explanation (for example, draftees into the army do not feel the same commitment as do volunteers in the Marine Corps).

Explanations of why such treatment results in intensified commitment generally involve some variation (or combination) of cognitive dissonance, self-esteem, or attribution theory in social psychology. The explanation goes something like this: most people are biased in the direction of wanting to think well of themselves and wanting others to think well of them also. If one volunteers to engage in humiliating or extremely stressful behavior that is visible to others, especially others whose evaluations are important, the volunteer is faced with the dilemma of attempting to justify this behavior to both self and others. In other words, why do I engage in such bizarre, demeaning behavior? This question can be answered satisfactorily in a number of ways: the individual can decide that he or she is strange or temporarily deranged, but since this is an admission that one has lost control, it is not a likely option unless there are professional mental illness definers, such as psychiatrists, promoting such a definition; the individual can discount the importance of the behavior by defining it as a lark or a joke of some kind; or the behavior can be interpreted as a sign of worth and the value of the group upgraded in an effort to make the demeaning behavior actually seem like a glorious event—for example, the Marine who successfully completes boot training is certain that the whole experience was a character builder and that the Marine Corp is an elite troop of "real men." When the individual is initially attracted to the group, this last answer to the question of why an ordinarily sensible person would engage in unsensible behavior seems the most likely one.

Public tongue speaking, at least in its initial manifestations, can be a humiliating experience, involving a surrender of a good deal of personal pride and dignity. CCR spokespersons are well aware of the value of this type of public humiliation:

> But even more significantly, tongues usually turns out to be the gateway to the charismatic dimension. It builds a person's faith in a concrete way. It gives him a clear experience of what it means to have the Holy Spirit work through him. . . . Yielding to tongues is an important first step, and it is worth putting effort into encouraging a person to yield to tongues, even to run the risk of being labeled "imbalanced" (S.B. Clark, 1973:147).

The term "being broken" crops up fairly regularly in the CCR literature (it is borrowed from Watchman Nee, 1965). Essentially it means that one must be broken to self, or completely surrender self-pride, before one can establish an authentic personal relationship with Christ. Tongue speaking is an exercise in brokenness and reflects the neophyte's initiation into the CCR.

In the context of pentecostalism, glossolalia is not interpreted as weird behavior. It is viewed as evidence that the Holy Spirit is speaking through the individual. Because glossolic behavior is anomalous and a bit bizarre, it generates an aura of mystery—why else would one be interested in it? "For them (100 nuns), the first message spoken in tongues was one of the most significant events of the meeting because it graphically demonstrated that what was happening was beyond the merely human level" (Cavnar, 1975:14). Most tongue speakers tell about the feelings of ecstasy that accompany the initial ventures into glossolalia. It should come as little surprise that the neophyte glossolalic experiences a "rush of warmth" or a "tingling like electricity" in the context of anticipating a personal visit from the spirit of God, intense group feedback, and the expression of a novel and anomalous behavior in public. This positive, intense emotional experience also helps commit the individual to the CCR. However, as with all intense emotional feelings, routinization erodes them. Various books and articles emanating from the movement warn the neophyte about the letdown which is inevitable and which encourages increasing involvement in prayer group affairs and in regular personal prayer to sustain the individual's commitment.

The initial experience of tongue speaking is a dramatic demonstration of the neophyte's commitment to the norms and goals of the CCR. This commitment brings intense personal rewards, as leaders and other group members gather around the initiate and offer congratulations while administering hugs, handshakes, and enthusiastic expressions of "praise the Lord." The initiate is now viewed as a full-fledged member and receives the attention and status commensurate with full membership. This increase in social rewards also increases commitment to the group and to the larger organization.

Glossolalia is a superb method of heightening individuals' perceptions of value and power and of committing them to the organization. To anyone who may be feeling lost or powerless in their relationships at work or with friends, spouse, or children, the reactions accompanying glossolalia can be rewarding indeed. A substantial flow of tears from the initiate is not uncommon at this point, reminiscent of a loving homecoming after a prolonged absence.

Interpretation of Tongues

Still another aspect of the tongue speaking phenomenon serves to increase control and commitment: the gift of interpretation of tongues. Leaders in the CCR are aware that even among its sympathizers, the emphasis upon the gift of tongues as an expression of the Holy Spirit poses something of a burden for the otherwise intellectually oriented follower. After all, it is not cynical to recognize that what is actually produced when one speaks in tongues is gibberish, or at the least, foolish and unintelligible sounds. (The Apostles were accused of being drunk.) Leaders readily acknowledge that glossolalia strikes against a conventional approach to receiving a word from God. Thus the matter of interpretation is of particular importance. Aside from its commitment function, a message from God in a language no one understands is of little value to the larger community.

Several observers (Sherrill, 1965; Samarin, 1972) have commented that interpretations of glossolalia offered in meetings are not very profound. Sherrill in particular was impressed by the feeling that interpretations often seem to come because Paul insisted on it (I Corinthians 14:28). For example, in one meeting there was an extended and vigorous singing in tongues by one individual, which was followed by an extraordinarily long and silent pause. The meeting then resumed for some 15 to 20 minutes with additional singing, praising, sharing, and other activities. Finally one member quietly remarked that no interpretation had been given of the message sung in tongues and looked expectantly toward the leader. Obviously unprepared for this, the leader, in a barely audible voice, interpreted the message as meaning "peace is always there. It is endless. Peace, my children, is within an arm's reach—take it." Our observations support those of others, in that all of the interpretations we heard were nearly identical to what is offered as prophecies in meetings: we should love one another; we should be open to the spirit; Jesus is going to do great works through us; and similar themes. These kinds of interpretations and prophecies serve to sustain and reinforce desired definitions of reality. CCR leadership applies the term "uplifting the community" to refer to this function; this is descriptively appropriate. This function will be further discussed in the next section on prophecy.

Aside from generally reinforcing group definitions of reality, interpretation of tongues can be used as a much more explicit control mechanism. For example, at one meeting we attended and taped, a large meeting in a Southern community, the following testimony was offered by an adult male about 35 years of age: "Jesus, I love you, and I know you love me. Sometimes you just tee me off! You just stand there." These words provoked one of the most spirited debates we witnessed in any of the prayer meetings in which we participated. The meeting had proceeded along familiar lines of hymn singing, prophesying, sharing, and tongue speaking. Following the "word of prayer" session, the man described above stood to share his problem with the group:

> There is something I would like to tell you. Right now, physically, I feel rotten. I have felt physically miserable for three weeks. Multiple sclerosis is an insidious and cruel disease. It is like the ancient English form of

torture and execution: drawn and quartered, where you cut off the arms and legs systematically and then finish the job. Multiple sclerosis is like that for some people, and it appears quite likely that the disease has attacked some nerves in my brain cells. It has made me feel sick in my stomach for the past three weeks.

Many times when people get up and speak in this group they speak from the side of the mountain, but I want to speak to you from the pit. And we can see into the pit in many people's lives as we look into the prayer requests that come into this group. And, from the pit I don't feel like being here. I didn't want to come tonight, but I'm here. And I just want to say, Jesus, I love you and I know you love me. Sometimes you just tee me off! You just stand there."

At this point the speaker was interrupted by another member of the group, a male of approximately the same age, who literally burst forth in a loud and compelling message in tongues. When he finished, the tongue speaker's wife immediately offered an interpretation: "It is not I who tee you off, but Satan." Following this interpretation the tongue speaker took off again. Then came the second interpretation: "It is he who is drawing [*sic*] you sick." The multiple sclerosis victim, still standing, said, "I couldn't hear you." A pronounced pause and silence came over the group, and finally the leader said that the interpretation was that it was Satan who was making him sick.

In an obviously tension-filled moment, the following interchange took place between the multiple sclerosis victim and the member who had spoken in tongues:

Tongue speaker: "Haven't you, haven't you . . . er . . . been prayed for before?
M. S. victim: "Oh yes, many times."

Tongue speaker: "Are you healed?"
M. S. victim: "I believe I am."

Tongue speaker: (in a very low voice) "Sit down, sit down. It's manifest. You just haven't seen it, that's all."

At this point the leader of the group indicated that the speaker should continue sharing with the group. A pause ensued, and the M. S. victim quietly said, "I'm finished," and sat down.

Following this dramatic encounter, a series of rapidly given sharings followed. All centered upon the theme that many people are mentally, spiritually, and physically ill, and that we should turn to Jesus for help. Stress was laid upon the fact that even when we do not understand, we should submit ourselves to the Lord and trust in his mercy. One woman stressed that she, too, felt "very rotten, mentally, not physically. There's not an ounce of love in me tonight and I really feel terrible. I hate myself for it, I really do. I know it's Satan, and yet I can't shake it—I'm too weak. I would like for everyone, please—let's just pray—if Satan is in anybody's mind, let's get him out—please, for everybody's sake."

Very intense group prayers and tongue speaking followed. The entire thrust of the meeting then centered upon "driving Satan out" and calling upon Jesus to come and be very real in the meeting. As the meeting drew to a close, the multiple sclerotic once again rose and spoke quietly. He stated that he had "received a signal from Satan to sit down and be quiet, but "now I feel moved to get up again and finish what I was going to say." If this message was intended as a direct attack upon the individual who delivered the message in tongues, it received no response. What ensued can only be described as an abject confession to the group asking for reinstatement to their good favor. His second statement accented the fact that he knew God had indeed healed him and was calling him to a task which perhaps no one else in the group could do. His suffering, he emphasized, called for great faith on his part which, he acknowledged, was not always present. But his love for Jesus and his knowledge that Jesus loved him would enable him to be sustained through this trial in his life.

The control aspects of this incidence are painfully obvious. The result was a desirable one in terms of group goals. The errant brother recanted his error, admitted his failing humanity, and reaffirmed his faith. Although this incident was by far the most blatant attempt at control, through tongue interpretation, which we observed, analogous events using both tongue interpretation and prophecy were observed. The message given in prophecy or tongue interpretation has a powerful impact, since its source is believed to be the Holy Spirit. Since it is from the Holy Spirit, the message is generally not critically analyzed and is not divisive to the group. This vehicle method of norm setting and sanctioning is an excellent way of ensuring norm conformity and dampening potential group conflict. As long as the tongue interpretation or prophecy is viewed as authentic, it must be accepted as God's word, and the transmitting individual cannot be held accountable.

We have already mentioned the parallel functions served by tongue interpretation and prophecy. It is to this latter phenomenon we now turn.

Prophecy

Prophecy may be the most misunderstood term in the lexicon of Christian and Jewish theology. The average layperson thinks of prophecy as some announcement of a future event, for example, the prediction in the Old Testament of the birth of Christ. But the prophetic message is best understood as a word from the Lord, for instruction or edification. This is the meaning which characterizes prophecies in the prayer meetings.

A prophecy may follow a period of silence, and is unannounced. It typically opens with the words "My people" or "My children:"

> My people, I ask you to come and taste and see; come and taste and see the light I reveal; come and examine the fruits of the Holy Spirit. I ask that you yield yourselves to me. I ask you to trust me, to open your hearts that I may enter your lives and change those lives. I ask that I might put into you the fullness of my Holy Spirit.

> I love you with a love beyond your comprehension; an infinite love which surpasses all things and which I long to share with you. Open your hearts and accept me as your Lord Jesus; trust me; I will do great things for you. You are my brothers; I call you into the fullness of your sonship with the Father. Praise the Lord.

Such prophecies are ordinarily delivered in a low key, without any effort to mimic the thunderings of an Amos or Jeremiah's "Thus saith the Lord!" If anything, they are sometimes difficult to hear in a large school auditorium. One movement leader admonished the prophet to "speak loudly enough for all to hear, but not so loud as to frighten anyone" (Cavnar, 1974:27). Prophecies are an integral part of the meeting, and two or three, at least, are generally offered at each meeting.

Presumably anyone may offer a prophetic word. This would be consistent with the value that the "spirit speaks where he wills." However, our observations strongly suggest that such activity is restricted to a select few, and is at times carefully orchestrated rather than being truly spontaneous. Articles in *New Covenant* and instructions given in the *Life in the Spirit Seminars: Team Manual* (S.B. Clark, 1973) clearly indicate that it is quite acceptable, even desirable, to preselect those who are to give prophecies during the prayer meeting on a given evening. Furthermore, there often is premeeting agreement on the general theme the subsequent meeting is to take so that the content of the prophecies is somewhat predetermined.

The most vivid orchestration of prophecies we witnessed occurred at the 1973 International Conference held at Notre Dame University. Before a prophecy could be delivered to the assembly it had to be written out; given a preliminary blessing by a "second in command"; and, if it survived the intial screening, it was passed on to the convention director, who then decided whether or not it could be delivered. At one point during the initial meeting in the Fighting Irish stadium on Friday evening, a Jeremiah type of prophecy began emanating from the upper decks of the southeastern section of the stadium. Clearly the would-be prophet had not gone through channels. The convention director handled the situation with admirable aplomb. He simply asked the assembly to pray and soon the voice of the would-be prophet was drowned out by thousands of people praying aloud and speaking and singing in tongues. It is significant that we never again witnessed an attempt to give a nonapproved prophecy at an international convention. While this degree of control might seem excessive, it has been publically defended by CCR spokespersons (*National Catholic Reporter*, August 1975a:3).

If one understands the role of prophecy in such movements, then the control of their utterances by the leadership makes sense. Prophecy is a principal way of affirming the authenticity and legitimacy of the movement, and of providing some uniform direction to the disparate groups across the country, even throughout the world.

Movement leaders writing about the role of prophecy stress that its purpose is to uplift the community and not bring dissension or conflict. Judging from the many prophecies we have recorded and those that are found in the pages of *New Covenant*, "uplifting" can be translated as an affirmation that the movement is truly of God and is guided by the active hand of God. In addition uplifting includes assurances that God will continue to provide strength, power, and eventual glory to believers. The following prophecy illustrates these functions well:

> Know that I, your God, brought Peter and Paul to Rome to witness to my glory. I have chosen you also and have brought you to Rome to bear witness to my glory, confirmed now by your shepherd. Go forth to the healing of the nations. Knowing that I am with you; and though you may pass through tribulation and trial, I will be with you even to the end. I am preparing a place for you in glory. Look to me and I will deliver you from the power of the evil one. Behold I am with you now, all days, even till the end of time (*New Covenant*, July 1975).

Similar prophecies delivered during prayer meetings assure members that their endeavors are inspired, guided, and legitimate.

However, prophecies also serve an important purpose for the wider organization of disparate groups. Prophecies delivered at international, national, and regional conferences set the general direction for the movement as a whole. These prophecies can be considered forms of organizational directives. In most cases these prophecies originate from and are discussed in the pages of *New Covenant*. They set the direction and tone for prayer groups throughout the world. Compare the following prophecies delivered at international conventions and place them in the context of a movement just coming into its own (1973); a movement more mature, confident, and self-assured (1974); and a movement beginning to have doubts, realizing that it is not going to conquer the world in the near future (1975):

> I am the Lord. I am present with you here. I am the Lord, and I have chosen now to act. I will awake this world to hear my voice. I will awake this world to hear the voice of its Lord, the mighty King. And I will speak my words of everlasting love to the hearts of men. And they will turn their hearts to me, and men will come to me rank upon rank. I will win them back with my tender affectionate love, and they will come to me rank upon rank and ask me for salvation, and I will grant it to them and grant them eternal life. I am the Lord, I have begun to act. I will pour out my Spirit with power upon the face of this earth, and I will clothe my servants with power and with a spirit of holiness so that men will see and know that I am at work in the world now. And where my name is not known and my name is not honored, I shall receive glory when men turn their hearts to me. I am the Lord, I have decided to act. I will do this: I promise it, I will do it (*New Covenant*, October 1973).

> I believe that God is saying that it is time to speak out his word boldly. He has a word to speak for the Church and for the world through what we are experiencing. Renewal is too weak a word for what needs to happen in the Christian Church. "Renewal" can give us a sense that we will just polish something up a little bit. Rather, I think God is moving to *restore* New Testament Christianity to all his people—that is more than renewal . . . He wants to change the face of the Church and the face of the earth . . . Today, if we love the Catholic Church as it is so much that we won't let Jesus make it what he wants it to be for today, we become the enemy of the Catholic Church (Martin, 1974:6). (This quotation is from an address delivered at the 1974 International Conference. While not a prophecy in the formal sense of the term, the editors of *New Covenant* refer to the address as "A Prophetic Vision," and other leaders concur.)

> Because I love you, I want to show you what I am doing in the world today. I want to prepare you for what is to come. Days of darkness are coming on the world, days of tribulation . . . Buildings that are now standing will not be standing. Supports that are there for my people now will not be there. I want you to be prepared, my people, to know only me and to cleave to me and to have me in a way deeper than ever before. I will lead you into the desert . . . I will strip you of everything that you are depending on now, so you depend just on me. A time of darkness is coming on the world, but a time of glory is coming for my people (from a prophecy delivered at the 1975 International Conference; reported in *New Covenant*, July 1975).

Each of these prophecies, or prophetic messages, emanated from the key leadership of the CCR, presented a reflection of the movement as it existed at the time of the prophecy, and set the tone for the movement in the immediate future. They are the primary means by which the CCR leadership exerts control on the rest of the movement—by presenting it with a definition of the situation which reflects the goals of that leadership. These messages are discussed at prayer meetings, in casual conversation, and at leadership meetings all over the world.

Since prophecies are viewed as originating from the Holy Spirit, there is little criticism of their content. Any serious criticism of prophecies generally occurs before they are given to the wider public. Movement leaders are extremely cautious in what they permit to be given as prophecies. When a prophecy is publicly given that does not agree with goals articulated in the CCR, it is quickly denounced. For example, David Wilkerson prophesied at a meeting of Lutheran charismatics that the CCR would eventually be forced to break from the church. This prophecy was quickly questioned in the pages of *New Covenant* (Martin, 1974:11).

The functions of prophesies should be obvious at this point. First, they confirm the legitimacy and value of each prayer group's activities. Second, they offer encouragement and hope for more wondrous events in the future. Third, they are a means for a highly centralized movement to pass on its directives without appearing authoritarian or directive. Fourth, because they are viewed as the word of God, they are relatively free from serious criticism and thus keep organizational conflicts, cynicism, and criticism to a minimum.

Healing

While each of the gifts discussed above play an integral part in increasing each member's feelings of efficacy, the gift that is unparalleled in promoting feelings of control is that of healing. When pentecostals speak of miracles happening in modern times, they are usually referring to faith healings of some sort.

Healing has been part of the movement since its early days. However, publicity about healings and the unhesitant proclaiming of healings developed relatively late in the movement. Two important books, *Catholic Pentecostals* by Kevin and Dorothy Ranaghan (1969) and *The Pentecostal Movement* by Edward O'Connor (1971), give very limited treatment to healing as a mark of the movement. O'Connor notes that most prayer groups "do not seen to be preoccupied with the subject." Some CCR leaders may not agree that O'Connor's book is important. Some regard him as attempting to dilute the movement by underemphasizing its significance. Morton Kelsey's *Healing and Christianity* (1973), a detailed treatment of healing in the church throughout its history up to modern times, has no reference whatsover to Catholic pentecostals (Kelsey was a member of the faculty at Notre Dame when his work was published in 1973.) In 1974 Francis MacNutt published *Healing*, in which he stressed that it should be considered normative for Christians to expect to be healed of their sicknesses. By 1975 reports of healing in the movement were of sufficient magnitude to warrant detailed attention to the subject in *New Covenant* (March 1975). Much of this attention was a result of a dramatic mass healing event which took place at the 1974 CCR International Convention at Notre Dame. More will be said of this event in the next chapter.

As the CCR movement has matured, then, the gift of healing has come to the forefront. Evidence for this is provided not only by the CCR literature but by our own questionaire data. In response to the question, "Have you, or someone close to you, experienced the gift of healing?", 71 percent of our sample answered "yes," and 46 percent (457 people) mentioned particular cures they themselves had experienced. The breakdown of types of illnesses and conditions reported as healed is as follows:

24% Common maladies like colds, cramps, sprains, headaches.

23% Healing of a chronic condition for which medical evidence can be gathered, such as epilepsy, cysts, acne, anemia, kidney problems, heart ailments, and so on.

20% Nonspecific statement of healing, such as I had my eyes, back, or foot healed.

9% Diagnosed cancer.

7% Emotional problems of some type.

6% Leg lengthening.[1]

5% Healing of a chronic condition which may have psychosomatic origins, such as arthritis, asthma, rheumatism.

4% Broken bone.

2% Other, noncodable response.

A quick examination of these conditions demonstrates that, while many of these reports involve conditions which are quite likely to have psychosomatic origins, many others are much more difficult to place in that context.

The concern with healing is similar to the attention give to tongue

---

[1] I had an opportunity to observe a "leg lengthening" healing and must report in all honesty that it reminded me of a game we played as children, which involved impressing friends by holding out an arm or leg and using some muscle control to retract the limb slightly, and then announcing that we could make the limb longer and then do so by relaxing the appropriate muscles. Leg shortening or lengthening could clearly be related to stress and anxiety, just as headaches can be related to stress-shortened neck and head muscles.—Richard J. Bord

speaking. Healing, like tongue speaking, has a long history in the church. It is biblically based on the reported healings of Jesus and the Apostles, as well as those of other followers in the early church, Paul included. In fact the Bible seems to indicate the Jesus' claim to legitimacy was based in part on the many dramatic cures he effected, which gave concrete substance to his supernatural claims. Reports of healing apparently serve much the same function today as they did in those earliest days of the church. They are evidence that the Christian way brings a form of control over the environment that is unavailable to most individuals.

Like tongue speaking, healing has often been associated with the more marginal religious groups in western society, and has at times been so exaggerated as to strain the imagination of the faithful among Christians. Reports of miraculous cures have persisted through the years, but it is clear that in the main line Protestant bodies and the Roman Catholic Church, the issue has been, by design, muted. Indeed this gift has been so deemphasized that Kelsey (1973:224) concludes that "There is no theology which is accepted or approved by any major modern church which has a place for the direct action of God in any of the gifts of the spirit, healing included."

The churches have adopted their position of disapproval of nonmedical healing in the light of the sustained advances in medical science from about the middle of the nineteenth century. Medical science itself has a long history of struggle from folk practices, including much superstition, to the virtually sacred status it enjoys today. As medical science progressed and grew increasingly dominant in the treatment of illness, other forms of treatment, including faith healing, declined as an important source of relief for the vast majority of the population. Sickness and its cure became the prerogative of the medical doctor rather than the priest. This of course was a result of the tremendous success modern medicine has had in treating many of the conditions that plagued humankind.

However, in spite of the acknowledged supremacy of medicine, an interest in nonmedical healing has continued. (This is particularly the case in the nonwestern world, where shamans continue to treat far more patients than any other type of practitioner. Among many peoples, modern medicine is totally absent, and the only available physician is the shaman.) This interest has been heightened by the fact that members of the medical profession, especially psychiatrists, have initiated dialogue with the Christian community on the relationship between illness and the spiritual and mental condition of the patient (Frank, 1973). Indeed the churches' interest has, in the view of some, lagged behind that of the medical profession. Before the birth of the CCR, not only Protestant pentecostal bodies but main line Protestant churches had begun once again to address themselves to the issue of nonmedical healing in contemporary society (Bonnell, 1968). While Kelsey is correct in noting that there is no general theological endorsement of miraculous healings by any major religious body, there is a renewed willingness to entertain the possibilities of this ancient practice in the midst of modern medicine.

This interest in nonmedical healing among those who understand and utilize medical healing is not surprising. The tremendous strides in medical knowledge have been accompanied by professional specialization; and the doctor-patient relationship, an integral part of the treatment process, may have suffered some depersonalization along the way. The persistence of interest in nonmedical healing, and its recent increase among middle class, educated people in the established churches, may be seen as a part of the search for personal identity in a mass society. The patient, like the assembly line worker, wishes to be something more than a slot in a bureaucratic organizational chart. If he or she cannot find personal relationships in dealing with medical doctors, he or she may well turn to other, nonmedical sources for treatment. The CCR is a part of a much larger collectivity who are stressing the need to respond to others as whole persons. Thus healing is not only that of the body, but of relationships as well; this emphasis is prominent in Catholic Charismatic testimonies and writings.

In attempting to understand the renewed interest in faith healing, one should not overlook the gap between illness and available cures. In spite of the progress of modern medical practice, there are still many human ailments which have proven quite resistant to simple cures or palliatives: cancers of all kinds, heart disease, various kinds of problems of the central nervous system, diseases of the joints, and the plethora of mental-emotional problems that seem to defy classification and treatment. People with extremely debilitating or terminal illnesses will go to some lengths to find cures. That some of them would turn to religious solutions is hardly surprising.

When healings are reported, an obvious question inevitably arises concerning the authenticity of the reports. Can medical evidence be mustered to support healing claims? Isn't faith healing a form of anti-intellectualism or a rejection of science and technology which can work to the extreme detriment of the sick individual?

Actually the approach to healing by the CCR leadership has been both cautious and quite sophisticated. First, almost every treatment of healing found in the pages of CCR literature is careful not to juxtapose scientific medicine and faith healing. Both are viewed as gifts from God and can be used in conjunction with each other or separately. There are relatively few group sanctions which discourage the seeking of medical help. In discussions of prayer groups and communities within the movement's literature, one often finds admissions that some people come into the

movement because of deep personal problems which are beyond the
ability of CCR people to deal with. In such cases the afflicted individuals
are encouraged to seek professional help of some kind.

CCR leaders are well aware of scientific canons of proof and are very
careful not to make claims that dramatically extend beyond the limits of
their own data. For example, in response to the question of documented
healings, Father Frances MacNutt, formerly the leading spokesman on
physical healing, states:

> I try to document them but I am handicapped by the travelling nature of
> my ministry. I do encourage people to write and tell things that have
> happened to them. We get an average of two or three testimonies a day. If
> someone's healing sounds like it could be verified by a doctor, I write
> back and ask if the doctor involved could document what has happened.

> We have received a few verifications of healings from doctors, and I tried
> to give some record of these in my book. But doctors are often reluctant to
> verify healings. They are afraid of appearing to be too credulous and they
> also find it difficult and often impossible to verify healings according to
> the strict rules of scientific evidence (*New Covenant*, April 1976:16).

Of course, MacNutt is correct. If someone with cancer is being prayed
for and the cancer disappears, it is virtually impossible to unambiguously document the cause of the disappearance. Debilitating organic
difficulties, even cancers, often remit, and the medical profession is
unable adequately to account for these remissions. Oftentimes the afflicted individual will be taking medication in conjunction with the
prayers for healing. If healing occurs, the medicine is likely to be labeled
as the cause. It is not surprising that one medical investigator concluded,
after a rather intensive investigation of faith healing in several settings
and cultures, that he could not find a single instance in which healing
occurred as a clear result of prayer or divine intercession (Nolen, 1974).
However, the "proofs" of physical and emotional healing through prayer
that we encountered in our research are at least as impressive, as a body
of evidence, as some of the data that the social and psychological sciences use to support their own generalizations.

CCR spokesmen are also aware of the criticism that faith healing only
deals with conditions that are psychosomatic in origin. Their response is
a reasoned and logical one: since so much human suffering is attributed
to psychosomatic problems, isn't the amelioration of such suffering a
legitimate service?

> It thus matters little whether the sickness we are freed from is organic or
> psychosomatic in its roots. Any kind of sickness is sickness; any healing

from God can be received in faith as a manifestation of his love for us. It matters little whether our healing occurs suddenly or gradually, whether it is the result of a sovereign act of God or accomplished in conjunction with the use of medication and therapy. And in most cases it matters little whether medical science can document that a miracle has occurred or not: many sicknesses by their nature do not lend themselves to such documentation ("A God of Power: Testimonies from the 1974 International Conference on the Catholic Charismatic Renewal," *New Covenant*, March 1975:18).

Faith healers are often successful in treating people who have taken drugs of various types or placebos, or had psychiatric therapy, sensitivity or encounter group experiences, or other "scientific" approaches to such problems. For example:

For the last 16 years I have had to take medicine to stay awake. Without it I found that I could even fall asleep standing up! Once when I was unable to get my medication for three days, someone found me sound asleep on the church floor.

Just a few months before the international conference, my doctor consented to an increase of my dosage of medicine because my condition seemed to be worse.

At the Friday night service at Notre Dame I felt that the Lord wanted to heal me. He seemed to be saying "you believe that I am healing others; don't you believe that I can help you too?" I remember saying, "Yes, I do believe." But I knew that my healing would be confirmed only when I stopped taking my medicine.

The next morning when I woke up I knew the Lord wanted me to trust him and accept his healing. For the first time in sixteen years I purposely didn't take any pills. However, I was aware that it would take up to three days for the previous medicine to wear off and the healing to be affirmed. During the rest of the conference my companions prayed over me and encouraged me. I felt great.

I waited three months before relating the incident to my doctor. He was quite impressed. He couldn't explain why I didn't have a setback after I stopped taking the pills, because it takes two or three months for the thyroid gland to return to normal function. He said that my sleepiness could have been psychosomatic in origin. In any event, he admitted that the Lord had affected a healing that he himself had been unable to accomplish.

I haven't taken any medicine since the conference and I feel better than I have in years. I praise God who has removed my fatigue and filled me with his life (*New Covenant*, March 1975:20).

In a related vein, we have heard and read testimonies from individuals who stopped taking drugs of all types after being baptized in the spirit. These included alcohol, heroin, various chemical depressants and stimulants (including those prescribed by physicians), cigarettes, marijuana, and coffee.

Father MacNutt offers some fairly stringent critieria for methods of documenting healings.

> I think they need to be scrupulously honest; I don't know how else to put it. For instance, from my little acquaintance with medicine, I know that if a person says he is without pain, that does not provide conclusive evidence that he has been healed. People should say only what the evidence allows: this person is now without pain and we thank God for it. We trust that he is healed, but we'll just wait and see what the next report is on this.

> Written confirmation or testimonies from a doctor that a healing has actually taken place make excellent documentation. Ideally this would include the doctor's records on the patient both before and after the person was healed (*New Covenant*, April 1976:16).

Even if such criteria were met, and in some cases they are, the doubts of the skeptic would probably remain. And even if symptoms persist, as was the case of the multiple sclerosis victim mentioned earlier in the chapter, the believer may report that he has been healed. These have always been issues in the history of faith healing, and they continue to exist for the CCR.

In spite of the reasoned, flexible approach to faith healing taken by the CCR leadership, it is still possible that abuses could take place. People who require medical attention could neglect obtaining that attention because they believe a spiritual healing to have taken place. While this possibility exists, we are not aware of any instances in which it occurred. The relatively high educational level of CCR adherents generally mitigates against choosing completely irrational alternatives in problem solving.

Another frequent dilemma is how to handle the cases in which prayer for healing was given but healing was not forthcoming. A number of answers are given to this dilemma: continue praying—sometimes healing does not transpire until after an extended period of intensive prayer; the problem may be the lack of sufficient faith on the part of either the healer, the patient, or both—it is necessary to pray in confidence; there is always the "court of last resort" answer—who can know God's will? God may have good reasons for continuing the individual's suffering (*New Covenant*, April 1976:7).

A central function of divine healing is the role that such a belief plays in the total life of a Catholic Charismatic. One of the dominant features of the movement is the belief that God can meet any need of those who trust him. Thus a relief from leukemia (or the finding of lost luggage, as reported during one meeting we attended) reaffirm both God's continuing care and the belief that the living Christ is presently working through individuals. This heightened experience of personal worth and efficacy is the function served by all the gifts of the spirit.

Spirit Discernment and Deliverance

One of the defining characteristics of Penecostalism has been its literal belief in evil spirits (Elinson, 1965). The CCR shares this belief. Articles concerning the reality of Satan, spirit discernment, and deliverance can be found in the pages of *New Covenant* (Cirner, 1974; Martin, 1974; O'Connor, 1975). A workshop given at the 1973 International Conference at Notre Dame, entitled "Alcohol, Drugs and the Occult: Ministering to the Counter Culture," dealt almost exclusively with the reality of evil spirits and how to deal with them. One of the two directors of this session described how he had physically wrestled with an evil spirit and had bested it by invoking the name of the Lord after the spirit had hurled him to the ground.

As has been true of traditional Christanity, the relationship between human beings and evil spirtis is defined as a battle: "Satan is our real enemy. He fights continually to keep us from God and to bring us to his kingdom. This is important for Christians to know: whether we like it or not, we are engaged in a very real battle" (Cirner, 1974:5). Satan brings fear and anxiety, psychological and physical addictions, strong temptations which erode self-control, and concrete evils such as war, starvation, and political oppression. In other words, Satan limits freedom and control. Faith, prayer, and deliverance techniques help resist these dark forces and reestablish control. CCR writers are quick to state that Satan's power has limits, and that evil can have sources other than spiritual ones. One writer depicts two other sources of evil which can be independent of evil spirits as "our own flesh" and "the world," not creation in itself but rather the patterns of society (goals, ideals, values, and trends) which are in opposition to God's kingdom and can lure his people away from him (Cirner, 1974:5).

The gift of spirit discernment is defined as the ability to determine "whether the inspirations or impulses that come into our minds originate from God, Satan, or ourselves" (O'Connor, 1975, Part I). How does one accurately discern whether an inspiration is from the Holy Spirit? A number of guidelines are suggested by O'Connor. The first set of criteria

he labels "objective" ones. First, one must often set aside his or her own
judgment, since impulses coming from the self are often not of God.
"Charismatic inspirations . . . have the character of messages coming to
us from a course other than ourselves," and "consist simply in a loving
inclination to do such and such a thing, or to do it in a certain way"
(O'Connor, 1975, Part I:11–12). Furthermore, Scripture, the doctrines
and laws of the church (defined as "God's people"), and the "duties of a
person's state in life furnish helpful criteria by which to judge an inspiration" (O'Connor, 1975, Part III:31). Obedience to legitimate authority is
viewed as evidence that one is led by the Holy Spirit.

There are also subjective criteria which demonstrate that an inspiration is from the Holy Spirit. If one is acting in accordance to the will of
God, he or she should be at peace; "peace comes from being in right
order" (O'Connor, 1975, Part III:26). Actions should also be impelled by
love, since "whatever is from God is ultimately motivated by love"
(O'Connor, 1975, Part III:27). Hostile confrontations should be viewed
with suspicion. Being in right order with God also brings joy. "The note
of joy is often the one sign by which true holiness can be discriminated
from false" (O'Connor, 1975, Part 111:27). Finally, inspiration from God
should generate humility. Inspirations which generate pride are probably
from self or Satan and not from God.

If one examines these criteria carefully it is clear that they orient the
believer toward those in positions of legitimate authority and foster conformity while dampening conflict. Since prophetical messages and other
organizational directives presented at prayer meetings, conferences, and
communities are disproportionately produced by recognized leadership,
to judge an inspiration as being of the Holy Spirit is the practical equiva-
lent of saying it came from the CCR leadership. The messages emanating
from the leadership become messages sent by the Holy Spirit. Furthermore, it seems logical to assume that conformity with group norms, in
the context of an agreed-upon definition of reality, would generate feelings of peace, joy, and love. Those who conform and exhibit the ideals of
the CCR should be rewarded with affection and with other signs of
value. These social rewards should generate a sense of peace. Humility is
simply another guard against conflict, dissension, and critical evaulation
of those directing the movement. It is a further means of social control
which does not generate feelings of alienation.

In addition, battles with evil spirits serve much the same function as
all battles—they increase group feelings of solidarity. At one meeting we
attended, a young lady began screaming that it is "lies, all a pack of
lies." This was viewed as evidence of possession by evil spirits. The
group, under the direction of the man and wife who were the leaders,
and whose home was being used as the meeting place, gathered around

the young woman and began intensively praying for her while "laying hands" upon her. But she had great stamina and continued to protest for the better part of two hours. Eventually, however, the distraught woman quieted down and admitted her folly. The group credited itself with having driven out a demon, and the remainder of the evening was characterized by great joy and mutual affection and admiration.

In its battle with evil spirits, some elements of the CCR exhibit interesting preoccupations. In the 1973 International Convention Workshop cited above, and in some prayer groups and one community we visited, there was an almost obsessive fascination with occult phenomena. The lay leader of the convention went to considerable lengths to outline the dangers of fortune tellers, soothsayers, anyone who uses a crystal ball or tea leaves, anyone who reads card or palms, follows a horoscope, astrology, ouija boards, or graphology (handwriting analysis), all of which are seen as manifestations of evil spirits. His contention was that these are techniques used to place one under subjection:

> I think the most important thing to remember here is the horoscope, you can find it in almost every newspaper in this country . . . I've had people baptized in the Holy Spirit come to me and say, "I can't really get with it." I kept picking up a wizard spirit and I said, "what have you been reading?" She said, "I've been reading the horoscope" . . . This brings you under subjection, that's what it's intended to do.

This statement obviously disturbed one young lady, who at that point bolted from the room with tears flowing from her eyes. The lay leader nodded toward the retreating figure and said, "See what I mean?" Similarly, the leaders of a Christian community and large prayer group in the northeast told how members of the community had taken their children out of a Catholic elementary school after hearing that some of the teachers, including some nuns, were teaching astrology and white witchcraft to the children. They then organized their own elementary school with the cooperation of a local Protestant pastor, who donated the basement of his church. Community members who had degrees in education donated their services, and the school was soon given state accreditation.

To think that one can do something positive about poverty, hatred, war, and personal problems by fighting spiritual entities increases feelings of efficacy while demanding little from the concerned individual. Constant battle with an enemy increases group cohesion and feelings of value. Spirit discernment and deliverance, like the other gifts, increases an individual's perception of control over a hostile environment, dampens intragroup conflict, increases member commitment, and promotes the unchallenged authority of the CCR leadership.

Summary

Social movements that require an intensely dedicated membership must incorporate rituals which enhance individuals' perceptions of efficacy. Such rituals, however, also serve the function of providing the means to exercise social control over their practitioners. The various gifts of the spirit serve these dual functions well.

Tongue speaking, or glossolalia, is practiced by most CCR participants. Its practice requires that the individual publically behave in ways viewed as peculiar by the nonpentecostal society. The overcoming of fear and embarrassment, required to speak in tongues, can be viewed as an initiation ceremony that helps commit the individual to the group. Regular tongue speaking is both a sign to the individual that God has accepted him or her as a tool and a sign to the group that this is a member in good standing.

Oftentimes the unintelligible sounds of glossolalia are interpreted in conventional language. These interpretations usually take the form of assuring the group that God cares for them and is guiding them. Occasionally tongue interpretation is used as a specific injunction to erring members or the erring group as a whole. Since the interpretation is viewed as the expression of God's will, it can be a powerful source of social control.

Like the interpretation of tongues, prophecy is a superb method of stating group norms in a manner that legitimates them with the blessing of God. Prophecy is viewed as the word of the Lord, and its practice is rather closely regulated by group leaders. Prophecies given at national conventions and other important meetings become the de facto policy statements for the at large movement. The content of these prophecies is passed on through articles in *New Covenant* and through testimony and sharing at local meetings.

Faith healing is another dramatic affirmation to movement members that their efforts are divinely sanctioned. While most reported healings are of routine maladies, some very dramatic cures of serious illnesses are reported by CCR members, some of whom have doctor's statements to enhance their credibility. While faith healing is generally encouraged by movement leaders, conventional medicine is also viewed as an instrument of the Lord.

Finally, the discernment and deliverance of spirits also provides CCR members with perceptions of efficacy and can be used as a means of transmitting group norms. The delineating of what is evil provides normative boundaries and pinpoints targets for distrust and revulsion. This creation of a symbolic out-group enhances the perception of in-group solidarity.

6
Impression Management: The Relationship between the CCR and Its Environment

At this point we have considered a neophyte movement that has almost all the essentials necessary to promote continuity and growth. The embryonic CCR has a committed leadership, who have both goals and training for effective leadership, a pool of searching individuals who could find such a group attractive, official proclamations that serve to legitimate its activities, and a set of highly effective commitment techniques. One further aspect is necessary to ensure success: an effective public relations program.

If an emerging social unit is to have any hope of success, it must present itself to potential members and potential critics in a manner suggesting legitimacy, impeccability, and desirability. This is especially crucial in contemporary society, with its extensive, rapid, and explicit communication media. Impression management is as essential for a would-be successful movement as it is for a would-be successful job applicant.

We contend that the CCR leadership has shown extreme adeptness in constructing a definition of itself that is acceptable to the wider public and the church hierarchy. Some of these public relations maneuvers have come back to haunt CCR spokespersons but in general they have been and continue to be successful in presenting themselves. The reader should not assume automatically that these self-definitions have been arranged in a planned, Machiavellian manner. In certain instances public relations were an integral part of leadership planning; in others, such a blatant construction of reality is not so obvious. In any case, successful public relations is a must for any social organization, and as such, does not constitute grounds for condemning the CCR. The successes of the CCR are a result of careful planning by well-educated human beings who have an uncommon understanding of group dynamics.

Three major types of impression management are of particular concern here. First, there is a construction of reality in order to appeal to the general public, and particularly to potential members. The CCR wishes to encourage as wide a base of attraction as possible, consistent with its goals. Second, if the CCR is to have any realistic hope of renewing the Catholic Church—in the sense of creating important structural changes—then it must favorably impress at least some portion of the influential clergy. Careful courting of the clergy has been one of the hallmarks of the CCR. Finally, as the movement and its social environment experience critical changes, its public face must be adjusted to show those changes advantageously.

Impression Management I: Encouraging Membership Growth and Promoting Public Appeal

As previously noted, the CCR leadership defines Christianity as in its death throes as a result of attacks by and capitulation to secular humanism. Divided Christianity is seen as suicidal. It is not simply the Roman Catholic Church that is in trouble but Christianity in general. Real ecumenicism is an absolute necessity, not an ideal luxury. To pursue this goal effectively the CCR leadership has been faced with an incredibly difficult task: it must appeal to as wide a spectrum of Christianity as is possible without alienating itself from the parent church. The other side of this coin is equally true: the CCR has had to continue courting the favor of the church hierarchy without alienating non-Catholic Christians. They are, as the old colloquialism says, between a rock and a hard place. We will eventually make it clear that the CCR has not been able to please all of the people all of the time.

The CCR has done a remarkable job in favorably impressing Protestant neopentecostals and at least some classic pentecostals as is evident from their participation in national conventions and their contributions to the *New Covenant*. An interdenominational convention held in St. Louis, Missouri, in 1977 further dramatized the success of the CCR's ecumenical efforts. On that occasion classic pentecostals, Protestant neopentecostals, and Catholic pentecostals praised the Lord as a body, and even engaged in a display of Christian humility by literally washing the feet of some Messianic Jews who were present.

Equally important, the CCR has been successful in harmoniously joining people of different political leanings, occupations, age categories, and cultures. This integration of heterogeneous people has been one of the primary reasons for the success and growth of the movement. The fostering of smooth interpersonal relationships has been an explicit policy, one which Steve Clark and others have written about in some detail.

In 1973 we attended a seminar session for neophyte pentecostals led by Steve Clark at Ann Arbor, Michigan. During the session a young man asked Clark whether it was the duty of a recommitted Christian to work actively toward social change designed to improve various problems of injustice. Clark's reply mirrored the position taken in his article "Social Action: Strategy and Priorities" (S.B. Clark, 1972b): that when all men accept the Lord, then and only then will there be any meaningful world change. The young man persisted, arguing that such an eventuality was highly unlikely and suggesting that social protest was a more viable, short-run alternative. The inquiring neophyte also attempted to pin Clark down to a policy statement about racial prejudice and poverty, but he received essentially abstract statements of principle, reaffirming Clark's belief in the need to bring all to Christ.

This illustrates a striking aspect of most prayer meetings and group life among CCR people: an extreme reluctance to discuss anything that might introduce conflict. In fact, anything that threatens unity is viewed as fertile ground for the working of the devil (*Team Manual*, p. 30). Recall our description in chapter 3 of the prayer meeting where the multiple sclerotic who voiced doubts about a supposed cure he had undergone was immediately silenced by a tongue speaker who, with the leader, said that the M. S. victim's problems were the work of the devil.

The avoidance of conflict is explicitly addressed at various points in the *Life in the Spirit Seminars: Team Manual.* In the section describing the construction of talks given to aspiring CCR members, the team member, who is more or less a teacher, is cautioned that "it is important for the speaker to avoid arguments and controversies in his talk. He should be sympathetic with others and not critical; criticism should be reserved only for sin and inadequate ideas. People and groups, especially churches, clergy, and religious practices, should never be criticized" (p. 41).

The emphasis in the movement literature concerning interpersonal relations is on creating a positive, reinforcing atmosphere that will draw people closer together and strengthen their commitment to each other and the movement's goals. Clark (1972:79) advocates open expressions of affection, actions indicating honor and respect, service to others in even the most menial tasks, and positive and encouraging speech. *The Life in the Spirit Seminars: Team Manual* stresses unity among the pastoral team to the degree that they have "one mind and one heart together" (pp. 3–31). They are to display concrete expressions of love, humility, and service toward each other.

This harmonious interpersonal atmosphere is clearly something that attracts many newcomers. Over the years Dick Bord had a number of social psychology students who were interested in religious phenomenon attend campus prayer meetings for a term and then write up their observations. Without exception these students are struck by the degree of warmth and acceptance that is communicated among CCR participants; this closeness is the single feature that impressed all of the observers. They do, however, report varying degrees of discomfort at being so generously hugged; such open expressions of affection are generally frowned upon in our culture.

The resulting image of harmony appeals to potential members, people of other faiths, and inquiring clergy. It is difficult to be critical of such a positive collective experience; and it is precisely this quality of warm personal relationships and relatively tension-free public gatherings that have, at least initially, endeared the CCR to potential critics. It is also precisely this quality that is often cited as evidence that Christ is truly present in the movement (by their fruits shall you know them). This image is not left to chance, but is carefully and explicitly promoted by the movement leadership.

Another related characteristic of movement dynamics is a relative absence of the kind of preaching and moral exhortation that have often been marks of similar movements in the past. We do not mean to suggest that issues of morality are left entirely to the predispositions of individual participants. We simply have noted relatively little explicit treatment of behavior the church has traditionally considered moral or immoral. Certainly traditional sexual values (prohibitions against premarital and extramarital sex, stressing marriage as a lifetime commitment, emphasizing modesty in dress and acts, and conscious control of sexual impulses) are stressed in some of the CCR literature (e. g., Gavrilides, 1976). Also at least one antiabortion article has appeared in New Covenant (Dozier, 1973). However, fire and brimstone preaching about morality are not characteristic of the CCR. Nor have we noticed any reference to acceptable birth control techniques for married Catholics, an issue that has caused so much consternation in the Catholic Church.

Our own data demonstrate that there is a rather wide variation in CCR participants' attitudes about the moral issues that have preoccupied the modern church (see table 3 in chapter 1). When presented with the statement, "any method of birth control is acceptable for married Catholics," 62 percent disagreed, 25 percent took a noncommittal position, and 13 percent agreed. The statement, "the rhythm method of birth control is the only acceptable method of regulating family size for married Catholics" elicited 31 percent agreeing, 30 percent taking a noncommitted stance, and 39 percent disagreeing.

Some confusion may be engendered by the statement that abstinence is permissible according to church teaching, although not advised, and that there are "natural" methods that are not strictly rhythm methods—the Billings method, for example. However, although our respondents were never reticent about adding comments at places on the question-naire that somehow displeased, confused, or misrepresented them, not one commented on this particular item.

This attitudinal variation among CCR participants not only reflects a general secularizing trend among Roman Catholics, but it also shows that this is not something the CCR leadership has felt worthy of much attention. Again, if one is seriously attempting to unite committed Christians, it is probably an optimal strategy to focus on those moral issues that most biblically based Christians can agree with and to simply ignore those that might be divisive or viewed as purely Catholic issues. The presentation of the CCR's moral stance has been such as to alienate as few committed Christians as possible.

One does not find in the CCR an emphasis on strict, extremely ascetic life styles. It is true that some CCR members have adopted very ascetic life styles, and in the convenanted communities simplicity is the order of the day. In some communities we visited we saw no television, few personal belongings, simple food, an early to bed and early to rise policy, and no secular magazines or newspapers. (The absence of secular magazines and newspapers does not completely shut the community member off from the world events. One household had an' official news condenser who, at the evening meal, was asked to reiterate the important news of the day. He very eloquently discussed some events in the Middle East, some of Richard Nixon's difficulties, and other national events. We inquired as to why this individual was saddled with such a responsibility and were told that he was particularly intellectual and was able to get at the heart of important issues. This confirmed our personal impression of the man.) On the other hand, we have drunk beer with CCR members, watched football games and played cards with them, and even sat around "pickin and singin" Woody Guthrie songs with a talented young pentecostal in a household in Ann Arbor. This degree of flexibility has not been left to chance. *The Team Manual* tells us: "Our objective is to avoid all puritanism. People may decide it is better not to smoke or drink or take drugs. We do not want to say that something is incompatible with Christianity when the Lord did not say it was incompatible" (p. 140).

The point seems clear. The objective of the CCR, as viewed by a dominant component of its leadership, is to bring as many people as possible to an experiential relationship with Christ. To accomplish this end the leaders concentrate on getting people committed to a set of interpersonal relationships with already renewed Christians, and they deemphasize anything that would be needlessly divisive. Once people become involved in intense interpersonal relationships with already renewed Christians, they will come under an effective system of norms and sanctions that will shape behavior in desired directions.

The public face that the CCR leadership has evolved has been very effective in attracting people from diverse religious, sociopolitical, and generational backgrounds. The emphasis is on flexibility and acceptance, not doctrinaire stances and exclusion. Whether or not this degree of acceptance can be maintained is a serious question and will be addressed in the next chapter.

Impression Management II: Courting the Hierarchy

To say that the CCR leadership has engaged in a heroic struggle to present an acceptable, undeniably within-the-church image to the hierarchy would be an understatement. From the beginning, Clark, Martin, and others have been acutely aware of the necessity to market the CCR as something that is neither strange nor new, but rather something that is strongly bound to Christian and Catholic Church tradition.

At the very beginning the CCR leadership attempted to establish cordial, cooperative relationships with local pastors; however, they found this to be a singularly frustrating experience because pastors were quick to see possible infringement on their own sovereignty and were unable to appreciate what the young pentecostals were attempting to do. It was soon recognized that acceptance would have to come from the top of the church hierarchy before it would have any kind of significant impact on the parish priests.

Unofficial liaisons were then established to inform bishops of Charismatic activity within their jurisdictions. These liaisons were instituted by the charismatics and not by the bishops. In some instances bishops were regularly sent newsletters that gave accounts of Charismatic activity and portrayed the participants in a desirable Catholic light. Church officials were often extended standing invitations to attend prayer groups and covenanted communities to see for themselves the "fruits of the Spirit."

In general, these efforts to establish legitimacy have been quite successful. On October 10, 1973, a contingency of CCR leaders, including Ralph Martin, met with Pope Paul VI in Rome. The Pope's remarks were very encouraging, although marked with notes of caution.

> We rejoice with you, dear friends, at the renewal of spiritual life manifested in the Church today, in different forms and in various environments. . . . (The Pope then listed a series of effects the CCR was having on participants that contributed to more effective Church involvement. However, he sounded an equally vigilant note.) The spiritual lives of the faithful . . . come under the active pastoral responsibility of each bishop in his own diocese. It is particularly opportune to recall this in the presence of these ferments of renewal which arouse so many hopes.

Even in the best experiences of renewal, moreover, weeds may be found among the good seed. So a work of discernment is indispensable . . . [and this discernment is the responsibility of] . . . those who are in charge of the Church (*New Covenant*, December 1973).

We were in Ann Arbor the day after Ralph Martin returned from this trip to Rome. The people we met in the Ann Arbor community, and those staffing the *New Covenant* office, were beside themselves with joy because of this event. Their desire to be accepted by the hierarchy was obviously genuine. However, this desire for acceptance was tempered by the leadership's desire to keep the CCR primarily a lay movement. The impression we received from our interviews with the Ann Arbor leaders (we were not permitted an audience with Steve Clark) was that clerics were more than welcome to come, observe, and paticipate, but they were not to be accorded positions of influence simply because they were clerics.

That the vast majority of CCR participants share in this concern for official acceptance was evidenced by the enthusiasm exhibited at national conventions each time a leading cleric took the podium. Standing ovations were the common responses to the cardinals and bishops introduced to the assemblies. Furthermore, a full 80 percent of our sample indicate that they think it would be helpful if more clerics were involved in the movement.

Each year of the CCR's history has seen a growing number of clerics participating in prayer meetings and national conventions, and assuming various leadership positions. In 1975 the American bishops formally acknowledged the CCR, and many of them established official liaisons between themselves and prayer groups within their jurisdiction. Clearly, the concerted efforts of the CCR leadership to gain official acceptance had paid off. In this official acceptance, an important role has been played by one particular prelate, Cardinal Leon Joseph Suenens of Belgium, in presenting an acceptable image of the CCR to the Vatican and in adding an aura of respectibility through his own participation.

One continuing and acrid critic of the CCR, Dr. J. Massyngberde Ford, associate professor of theology at Notre Dame, has implied that Cardinal Suenens's support of the CCR is a result of his having been manipulated by the CCR leadership. There does exist sufficient evidence to indicate that the face of the CCR initially presented to the cardinal was indeed carefully orchestrated. However, we do not think this incidence of manipulative self-presentation is sufficient to explain the cardinal's support for the CCR. The cardinal's own long-standing goals and problems meshed very nicely with what the CCR was doing. One can be viewed as the complement of the other. Before elaborating that point, we will discuss the planned manipulation incident at the True House community during Cardinal Suenens' visit to Notre Dame in 1973.

Some of the events we are about to discuss have been mentioned in the national and Catholic press (see *National Catholic Reporter*, August 15, 1975 and have been partially rebutted in *New Covenant* (November 1975: 22–23). The rebuttal essentially argues that the facts of the case were not sufficiently investigated, that the complainants were disaffected members and therefore not credible witnesses, that the community in which the events occurred has since disbanded, and that those events were not characteristic throughout the movement. The latter two points seem to us to be generally true and will be treated in greater detail in the next chapter. We were aware of these incidents almost as they happened. We had close friends in positions of authority in that community and talked to members who at the time were not disaffected at all. In fact, at the time these events were narrated to us, the narrators were jubilant about the degree of success their community was enjoying. Over drinks in a private home in South Bend, Indiana, one evening after a general session during the 1972 convention, we offered the opinion that the degree of outright manipulation characterizing the True House community was unhealthy and boded ill for its future. At the time our hosts downplayed our concern, but one year later, after discovering that they too were on the receiving end of the manipulation process, they abandoned the renewal in shock and disgust. However, at the time of the events at the True House community at Notre Dame, they were high placed members in good standing. Two influential CCR members who had originally been involved in the Notre Dame community, Kevin Ranaghan and Paul deCelles, split from the campus group and formed their own People of Praise community in South Bend. The People of Praise community is modeled after the Ann Arbor community and is considered one of the more successful existing communities. Ranaghan was the only individual we encountered in our research experience who absolutely refused to talk to us. The report was that he was fed up with researchers. However, he did send someone to talk to us, and some questionnaires were distributed within that community.

The individual who headed the True House community was until 1973 an influential CCR leader who had originally been a friend of Steve Clark, had contributed to the movement literature, and who had been heavily involved in organizing the early national and international conventions. He has subsequently left the movement. It was he who was apparently primarily responsible for the manipulative atmosphere of the Notre Dame community. (This individual and Steve Clark experienced a cooling of their friendship. One informant told us that "the two egoes could not take each other.") For example, when arrangements were being made to purchase property for what was to be the True House community, adjacent property owners began organizing a protest over the intrusion of these religious "weirdos." A neighborhood picnic was organized by the True House leaders to get the two factions together. Only the most articulate, attractive, and impeccably well-behaved pentecostals were selected to attend. They were told which topics to discuss and which to avoid. The whole picnic was designed to create the desired image. The event was successful, and the property was purchased by the Notre Dame group.

A similar but more elaborate orchestration took place when Cardinal Suenens visited Notre Dame in 1973. Our sources for this information were three members of the community. Again the effort was devoted to creating as positive an image of the pentecostals as was possible. Only the most stellar examples of CCR membership were allowed near the cardinal. During a reception for the cardinal, a loose but effective protective ring of bodies shielded him from persons deemed by the leadership to be intrusive or unacceptable. If such a person attempted to approach the cardinal, he or she would be intercepted by one of the body guards and led off to the punch bowl or to some area where little harm could be done. The entire visit was preplanned and controlled to a remarkable degree. The phrase "create an artificial environment" was used by the Notre Dame leadership to characterize what was happening. The cardinal was not aware of the orchestration.

He left the Notre Dame community with a positive image of the CCR leaders. However, to assume that it was the creation of that "artificial environment" that committed him to the defense and support of the CCR is naive indeed. Cardinal Suenens and the CCR were made for each other. Suenens is a liberal prelate who, among other things, has expressed his hope and belief that science was close to perfecting a morally acceptable birth control pill (it has yet to happen). During the Vatican Council's 106th general meeting, he advocated a more open and flexible relationship with atheists, and more recently, he took issue with the papal ban on formal discussions of clerical celibacy. (Suenens's positions on these matters are referenced in McCormick, 1964; Wallace, 1965; and Fesquet, 1970.) More importantly, Cardinal Suenens has long been a proponent of shared responsibility in the church—that is, shared between clergy and laypersons.

During the Second Vatican Council, which predated the CCR, Cardinal Suenens mounted a courageous campaign aimed at promoting consideration of the importance of the charismatic gifts for the modern church.

One of the unforgettable speeches of the Council was Cardinal Suenens' address on charisms. The Cardinal struck at the false notion that these

gifts of the Holy Spirit for the good of the Church were unessential phenomena in the life of the Church. "Do we not all know laymen and lay-
women in each of our dioceses . . . endowed with various charisms of the
Spirit? Whether in catechetical work, in spreading the Gospel, in every
area of Catholic activity in social and charitable works (Fesquet, 1970).

This statement clearly indicates that the CCR did not manipulate the
cardinal into an interest in the charismata or the Holy Spirit. "I did not
discover the Holy Spirit through the renewal. As I have said, the Spirit
had long been at the center of my life" (Suenens, 1975).

The cardinal's interest in the charisms is related to his wish for more
democratic decision making at even the highest levels of the church. He
has attempted to present the church's primary mission as that of fellowship, not hierarchy, and has also dealt with the limits of papal authority.
His quest for shared responsibility has been singular enough to be characterized as a voice crying in the wilderness. "Is Cardinal Suenens a voice
crying in the wilderness? There is much evidence for fearing that as long
as the present administration remains in Rome, there will be no change"
(Baum, 1969). A focus on charisma for members at all levels justifies an
emphasis on shared responsibility. Shared responsibility is primarily
what the CCR is all about. Some long-standing goals of the cardinal and
the goals of the CCR are clearly identical; therefore, it would have been
unusual if Suenens had not risen to champion the CCR.

The cardinal's relationship with the CCR, however, is even deeper than
that between a person with a dream and an organization that gives
promise of realizing that dream. Like many Vatican II and post-Vatican
II clerics, Suenens was apparently experiencing grave doubts about the
ability of Christianity and the church to remain viable in the modern
world. The CCR has been a "shot in the arm" to some clerics on the
verge of despair and to Suenens himself: "I can say, I think, that I owe to
the renewal a spiritual youth, as it were, a more tangible hope, and the
joy of seeing impossible things become possible" (Suenens, 1975).

Although Suenens has been the champion of the CCR, his support has
not been unqualified. For example, in an article reflecting on the accomplishments of the CCR during its first decade, Suenens repeatedly stresses
the continuity of the CCR with church tradition. "It is of the utmost
importance that the charismatic renewal maintain this sense of continuity and not create the impression that the renewal is coming out of the
blue to start radically new things" (Suenens, 1975). The fact that he feels
compelled to address this issue amply illustrates his awareness of the
possibility of elitism and schism inherent in such an organization. In a
New Covenant article, he argues against the idea that the CCR is a
movement separate from the church: "Is the renewal some sort of injec-

tion of new blood into the body of Christ, something coming from outside? No. There is no such thing as an institutional church in contrast to a charismatic church. There is only one church." (Suenens, 1977).

These types of remarks are not simply comments on the accomplishments of the first decade of the CCR; they are cautions directed at CCR participants. Cardinal Suenens is quite cognizant of potential threats the CCR poses to the institutional church.

Another way the CCR has presented itself as strongly prochurch is through articles and statements in *New Covenant*. There have been three classes of these prochurch articles. First are those written by clerics, which are essentially cautions to the CCR. Second are those articles that attempt to tie events common in the Charismatic Renewal with church tradition. Finally, a number of articles and statements have been issued by the CCR leadership which reaffirm the CCR's goals while attempting to place these goals squarely within the church.

Among the articles by clerics that are caveats to the movement is one written in 1973 by Bishop Joseph McKinney, Auxiliary of Grand Rapids, Michigan, and member of the Service Committee of the CCR, himself a Charismatic and involved quite early in the development of the CCR. This article was designed to further the integration and participation of priests in the movement. The bishop clearly regards clerical participation as a necessity to keep the CCR on the proper path: "There is no doubt in my mind that, when balanced priests are involved over a year or two with a prayer community, that prayer community is a deeper expression of the Church. We need shepherds, and priests are our most reliable source" (McKinney, 1973). Although the bishop apparently does not share the CCR leadership's enthusiasm for retaining the movement's primarily lay character, his letter was still published in *New Covenant*.

In a 1975 issue of *New Covenant* appeared an article by Cardinal Willebrands, who is president of the Vatican Secretariat for Promoting Christian Unity. The cardinal minces no words in establishing the church as the principal seat of the Holy Spirit:

> Brothers and sisters, I would like to ask the specific question: if the Spirit and the Church are so inseparable that the coming of the Spirit is the birthday of the church, could we ever separate the charismatic, the special gifts of the Spirit, from the church? The only solid and sound explanation of what is usually called the charismatic renewal in the church, is to be sought in the fact that the Spirit has been bestowed upon the church (Willebrands, 1975).

In other words, the CCR should not view itself as the originator of the charismata, as the giver of the gifts to the church; it must realize that

the charismati come from the church, via the Holy Spirit—a vivid asser-
tion of Church primacy.

In 1976–77 Killian McDonnell, a respected scholar of the CCR, contributed articles to *New Covenant* which warn Charismatics that their quest
for ecumenicity may lead to a "churchless Christianity" (McDonnell,
1976). He argues for the need to integrate the veneration of Mary into the
CCR, since by and large the CCR has not been a champion of Marian
devotion. The mention of Mary at prayer meetings is extremely rare, and
only 18 percent of our sample agree that "There should be more emphasis on Mary in prayer meetings." McDonnell (1977:29) views this as a
discontinuity in Catholic tradition and argues that Mary was "the first
charismatic."

> But if the Catholic Charismatic Renewal is not to restrict the Spirit, it
> needs to see in the whole historic experience of the church the footsteps of
> the Spirit. Over the centuries the experience of millions of Christians
> witnesses to the role of Mary.

Again, even though Marian devotions are not central to the CCR, the
leadership saw fit to publish this plea from a cleric to integrate Marian
devotions into the CCR.

The fact that the CCR leadership publishes critiques and warnings in
its principal periodical adds authenticity to their claim that they are "in
the church and for the church" (Martin, 1976). It would indeed be
difficult for critics and potential critics to argue convincingly that the
CCR has ignored possible sectarian issues.

New Covenant also publishes articles devoted to establishing unambiguously the perception of continuity between traditional Catholicism and
CCR beliefs and practices. For example, one article ties the CCR's emphasis on Satan to traditional Catholicism and the contemporary needs of
the Church (*New Covenant*, April 1974). Another issue of *New Covenant*
has two articles attempting to demonstrate that baptism in the spirit has
always been in the Catholic tradition. Essentially, these authors argue
that the spirit is initially received in baptism, but is given with renewed
intensity in such sacraments as confirmation and holy orders. So, it is
argued, issues of personal renewal are not new to Catholicism. Even
esteemed theologians are called upon to justify the CCR within the context of the institutional church. Father Heribert Muhlen (*New Covenant*,
July 1974) tells us that: "I think the charismatic renewal is God's response to what was called for in Vatican II as regards a more collegial,
brotherly, communal way of making decisions and exercising authority
in the Church."

Through the publication of these types of articles and features, the

CCR covers itself from charges of elitism and of attempting to introduce something new to a church which, by definition, already has the basics of everything. The CCR says that they are simply stressing what has been there all along.

The CCR leadership itself occasionally publishes position statements in *New Covenant*. These statements generally include specific attempts to cement, in the reader's mind, the perception of the CCR's loyalty to the church. Two articles in the January 1974 issue attempt to do this in a rather dramatic way (*New Covenant*, January 1974, 19–20; 21–23). A statement made by the Service Committee of the CCR concerning ecumenicism assures the reader that the CCR's comradeship with Protestants constitutes no threat to their Catholic allegiance:

> We recognize that, as Catholics, we are called to work for a unity among the followers of Christ . . . We are called to this commitment because we realize that the renewal of the Church will not be complete until a full and visible unity among Christians has been restored . . . At the same time, we are committed to our Church. This commitment is genuine and loyal, and we know that the Lord wants us to remain faithful to it. We recognize that the bishops of the Roman Catholic Church are over us in the Lord and that we should be subordinate to them (*New Covenant*, January 1974a:19–20).

In the same issue of *New Covenant* a statement of the CCR's theological foundation is presented. This statement, originally constructed at the 1974 International Convention in Rome at the instigation of Cardinal Suenens, reinforces the point that the renewal represents an emphasis in intensity and not in kind.

> Those within the charismatic renewal make no claim to a special spiritual endowment or to a special grace which distinguishes those involved in the renewal from those not so involved. If they differ at all they differ in awareness and expectations and therefore in experience. The purpose of the renewal is not to bring to the Church something she does not have, but to bring local churches and the Church universal to Jesus Christ, and to widen the expectations of how the Spirit comes to visibility in the charisms within the life of the Church (*New Covenant*, January 1974b: 21).

A final example of the CCR leadership publicly defending their pro-church orientation concerns a rather dramatic minor scandal in neopentecostalism. At the August 1973 International Lutheran Charismatic Convention, David Wilkerson (see chapter 4), publicly divulged the content of a vision he had experienced. Among other things, Wilkerson's

vision portends a time of persecution of Catholic Charismatics by the
official Church:

> The Roman Catholic Church is about to "pull in" the welcome mat to all
> Catholics who speak with tongues and who lean toward Pentecostal
> teachings concerning the Holy Spirit. High level political pressure will be
> placed on priests to "put the fire out." Watch for the Pope to take a
> negative stand against the charismatic movement within the Catholic
> Church. The honeymoon is over (Martin, 1974: "David Wilkerson's Vi-
> sions" p. 11).

Ralph Martin levies charges at Wilkerson of sensationalism and of purposely manipulating public opinion for his own ends. He quotes from a
biblical text which encourages the testing of prophecy to ensure its authenticity. In the same issue of *New Covenant*, the influential Protestant
pentecostal David duPlessis (1974) also deals with Wilkerson's vision and
urges careful discernment of spirits to avoid deception and falsehoods.

In Martin's and duPlessis's rebuttal of Wilkerson's "vision," it again
becomes apparent that prophecies which support the movement's goals
are deemed authentic, while those which are critical or potentially divisive are judged as not from God. This congruence between movement
goals and accepted prophecy is of more than passing interest and constitutes the last focus of our attempt to describe ways that the CCR adapts
to its external environment.

Impression Management III:
Movement Directives through Prophecy

It is essential that a developing movement be able to change emphases
as it experiences varying degrees and kinds of successes and reversals. A
social organization must be able to mobilize its members in desired
directions in order to facilitate goal attainment. This is a formidable task
for an organization such as the CCR, which is only partially structured
and is composed of geographically and culturally disparate, autonomous
groups. One way the leadership of such an organization can guide its
progress is to have its pronouncements considered as moral imperatives.
We suggest that the prophecies emanating from the CCR leadership have
the characteristics of moral imperatives that set the tone throughout the
entire movement. They are viewed as moral imperatives because they are
considered products of the Holy Spirit. The fact that movement leaders,
at various times and places, give prophecies having similar content is
taken as evidence that the prophecies are authentic. These prophecies are
published in *New Covenant*, audio taped and distributed to those who

care to purchase them, discussed at regional, state, and local meetings, and also disseminated through the informal communication networks that exist between national and international leaders. They set the tone for the entire movement.

The CCR leadership shares an intense and oftentimes intimate culture. There is a great deal of mutual discussing, sharing, and giving of testimonies. For example, during our visit to the *New Covenant* office in 1973 the entire staff dropped everything at a designated morning time and conducted a period of prayer and sharing. Many mutual trials and triumphs were here discussed. Leadership at all levels are constantly engaged in team or pastoral meetings to discuss critical issues. In other words, it is a culture in which ideas are rather freely and profusely shared.

In this atmosphere people find themselves thinking along the same lines about the same topics. As they pray, contemplate, and think about various problems, prophecies form in their minds which relate to these problems. As they give these prophecies, they are struck by their congruence of content. This congruence is then viewed as evidence that the prophecies come from the Holy Spirit. We would argue that they come from a shared culture and from minds working in similar directions. In any case, the more dramatic, congruent prophecies are then passed on to the membership, who view them as moral imperatives and use them to guide their own activities and form the themes that dominate prayer meetings all over the country. The more dramatic and congruent prophecies then become part of the wider CCR culture.

The prophecies we are about to discuss are viewed as benchmarks which indicate problems the CCR was trying to cope with at the time the particular prophecy was in ascendance. The change in their respective content indicates critical phases that the CCR has experienced. These prophecies and prophetic talks guided movement participants in ways which furthered movement goals. There are roughly three phases that can be abstracted from CCR development up to this point: the building phase, the triumphant phase, and the consolidation phase.

Prophecy: The Building Phase

The first six years of CCR development centered primarily on the establishment of an identity as respectable and church-loyal Christians. It was a time of continuing and dramatic growth and rising expectations. As previously discussed, the CCR was successful in attracting supports from church officials and from sympathetic Protestant pentecostals. During these first six years, the CCR took substantial strides toward becoming an ecumenical and international movement. This was a period of tentativeness, of groping, of advancing and retreating, of almost extreme humility. This was primarily the building phase.

This phase probably reached its culmination in 1972 and 1973. The June 1973 International Conference of the Catholic Charismatic Renewal at Notre Dame, Indiana, was an interesting mixture of the humble emphasis characterizing the first six years and the seeds of the triumphant phase, which was publicly expressed at the 1974 meeting at Notre Dame. In 1973 the number of conventioneers became too large to minister to in an available indoor facility. The 25,000 or more (estimates vary) people met for the first time in the Fighting Irish football stadium at the University of Notre Dame; both organizers and participants were obviously pleased by the size of their assembly. Also, the 1973 convention brought a relatively large European and South American contingency of participants. At one point during a general assembly, the non-North Americans were asked to rise and briefly identify themselves and their country. This ended with the assembly singing "he's got the whole world in his hands." Signs of success were everywhere.

The tone of the convention was dramatically set by the early speakers at the general session on Friday evening, June 1. A prominent Protestant pentecostal leader told the gathering:

> I believe that this is just the beginning, I think we are ready to enter one of the greatest moves of the Spirit that the world has ever had and ever seen . . . I believe at this conference we are going to see some of the greatest and the mightiest things that we have ever beheld.

A later speaker reinforced this theme even more dramatically by saying:

> this year the novena for Pentecost begins today, and this year of Pentecost begins a holy year proclaimed by our Holy Father Pope Paul VI, in which he expects the Spirit to move like a great wind over this whole land, so let us focus on Jesus . . . so he will fill us, not only us but the Church and the whole world with his Spirit like a living river.

This statement greatly moved the crowd, probably because it was interpreted to mean that the Pope's reference to the Holy Spirit was a signal to the movement to begin to change the face of the earth. After all, were they not the major church-related element to be placing primary stress on the Holy Spirit? The Holy Year was to be their year.

Later in the evening, the following prophecy was given:

> Oh my beloved children, if thou didst know the love that I am pouring forth in the deepest part of your being this night, if you would open unto

me the door that only you can open, if you but understood that gentleness of my love, the sweetness of my annointing, the tenderness of the Shepherd's heart wouldst thou not open unto me this night to receive the love that I freely give unto thee? For in this very hour I am among you to love you, and caress you with a love that shall consume thee. For this love is everlasting. It takes not account of the past, but of the present moment. For here my people, in your presence, I dwell, to receive you, to renew you in the deepest part of your being.

Turn your hearts now that I might begin in you the bearing forth of fruit of such sweetness and such magnitude and variety that my Church shall proclaim from high and from low the renewing work of the Holy Spirit among you. For you, my people, have been called forth this night into a great work of renewal. Give me your heart, for there it shall begin, and there it shall end, in the glory that my Father has placed within you.[1]

This prophecy, and the theme of all the events of the evening, was then clarified by one of the convention organizers: "This night, God has spoken a word to us . . . what central point shall I look at . . . there is going to be a great work, He is doing a mighty thing, a storm of his Holy Spirit." This prophecy, and another with the same general content (cited in part in chapter 5) were later printed in *New Covenant* magazine. The entire 1973 conference inspired the convention participants and those who later read and heard about these events to a belief that they were actually the mechanism chosen to bring about a genuine renewal in the Catholic Church. Past doubt and hesitancy was to be dissolved in a new confidence that the CCR was indeed God's tool to be used to reform the earth.

The 1973 conference also contained many cautions on potential pentecostal excesses and some vigorous reiteration of the CCR's loyalty to the church. The main speaker at the opening general assembly saw fit to warn participants:

> Another call of the Lord to us today is obedience to his representatives. . . . Obedience to church authorities has always been one of the genuine tests of what is truly of the Holy Spirit. If we are humbly obedient to our local bishop that is a sign that we are being led by the Spirit.

This call to obedience was later "confirmed" by a Scripture reading by one of the CCR's more illustrious leaders. Later speakers talked about the

---

[1]This verbatim transcript of our tapes differs slightly from the version printed in *New Covenant*, October 1973, p. 23, but this is word for word from our own tapes.

importance of reason and stressed that the Holy Spirit also works through the application of reason, is in addition to reason, and does not supplant it. Another addressed the assembly and told of the problems of "excessive enthusiasm" and "fanaticism."

Even though the 1973 convention had both optimistic and cautionary tones, later publications, like *New Covenant*, sought to stress the optimism. In order to help create a definition of reality that would encourage CCR participants, the triumphal elements of 1973 were stressed. This emphasis can be viewed as preparatory to the distinctive events of the 1974 convention.

Prophecy: The Triumphal Phase

The 1974 Notre Dame Conference was "a turning point," a move "from an apologetic phase to a prophetic phase" (Martin, cited in Jahr, 1974). The 1974 Eighth International Conference on the Charismatic Renewal featured an event that ordinarily would have generated horror in the Roman Catholic hierarchy. On the opening evening of the conference, under the direction of three priests, one nun, and a laywoman, an exceptionally dramatic and emotional healing service was conducted. The results of that service were viewed as ample confirmation of the biblical testimony that Christ made the blind to see and the lame to walk. One young woman, blind from birth, reported seeing those around her for the first time. Others reported healings of arthritis, cancer, blood problems, and kidney complications. Although this service aroused some concern among the more traditional Catholic laypeople and hierarchy, it was generally considered dramatic evidence that Christ was working in the modern world.

That this event could occur without an immediate negative reaction from the church hierarchy clearly indicated that the years of careful impression management had paid off. In 1974 the CCR unabashedly proclaimed its success and new self-confidence. During the main address, Ralph Martin decried the fragmentation of Christianity; announced that God was now in the process of uniting this ruptured edifice; told of witnessing Bishop McKinney giving a prophecy and of Cardinal Suenens singing in tongues; and then announced that "God is moving in an active, powerful way to renew the whole Catholic Church." Even more importantly, Martin (*New Covenant*, September 1974) essentially supported our main points concerning impression formation in the building phase when he said:

> Over the last five years God has given us great wisdom about how to relate to our fellow Catholic laymen and our Catholic bishops so that we

can all move together as a church. God has spoken to us about loyalty as Catholics and commitments of obedience and submission to our bishops. That has been a very important thing. Now with that as a foundation, I believe that God is saying that it is time to speak for the Church and for the world through what we are experiencing. Renewal is too weak a word for what needs to happen in the Christian Church. "Renewal" can give us a sense that we will just polish something up a little bit. Rather, I think God is moving to *restore* New Testament Christianity to all his people— that is more than renewal.

Here, then, was an unequivocal public statement of victory. The CCR was not simply a movement whose purpose was to add new vigor to the Roman Catholic Church; it was to be considered the harbinger of a new Christian world. The days of bowing and scraping were over; the day of triumph had arrived.

Martin's address had a profound impact on its listeners. Written comments (*New Covenant*, September 1974:7–9) by respected CCR leaders reflected that impact. One cleric wrote:

> I felt anointed during the whole of his talk. Is it renewal we are talking about or is it restoration. I know at times I go cold at the thought of what may lie ahead of us . . . Are we, like the sons of Abraham, too concerned with our roots, our Catholicity? Do we see union as others submitting to us, or can we envision it in wider terms, in the terms of God?
>
> We are approaching a moment of decision; God's call is more radical than we first supposed.

Another noted cleric termed the charismatic renewal "a sovereign act of the Father, restoring the Lordship of Jesus in the love and power of the Holy Spirit, in individuals, in the church, in Christianity, and in the world." Cardinal Suenens expressed the "hope that Ralph's address will be fully published in the *New Covenent* and that it will be inspiration for all the Fathers at the Synod in Rome this coming autumn."

This triumphal mood, however, was relatively short-lived. In 1975 the Catholic Charismatics returned to Rome to hold the International Conference at the seat of Roman Catholicism. On the last day of that conference the Pope addressed the conference participants at an audience held in St. Peter's Basilica (*New Covenant*, July 1975). The Pope's words were generally warm and encouraging, but they retained elements of caution. The closing paragraph of his official text is particularly noteworthy: "Beloved sons and daughters, with the help of the Lord, strong in the intercession of Mary, Mother of the Church, with your Pastors, you will be sure of not deceiving yourselves. And thus you will contribute, for your part, to the renewal of the Church." The Pope explicitly draws attention here to Marian devotion, which has never been an integral part of the CCR. He reminds his audience that they need pastoral counseling to avoid self-deception, and finally describes the group as partial contributors to church renewal. This could hardly be interpreted as a papal acceptance of the 1974 dicta that the CCR is out to restore "New Testament Christianity to all his (God's) people." In fact, the Pope's statement could be interpreted as almost condescending. Although his words were viewed as generally "warm, friendly, and clearly supportive" (Ghezzi, 1975), they revealed that he did not see the CCR in the same light as he apparently viewed traditional churchgoers.

Other trends became obvious in the period between 1974 and 1975. The CCR's rate of growth faltered for the first time. Obviously the bulk of Roman Catholicism was not going to embrace warmly the CCR. During this time the divorce rate for Roman Catholics approached that of the total population. Abortion was more accepted and had its share of Catholic supporters. If the CCR was indeed destined to restore the Church and the entire Christian world, it became manifestly obvious that it was not imminent. The euphoria generated by the signs, wonders, and speeches of the 1974 International Convention began to give way to some realistic pessimism.

So, although the 1975 convention at Rome was a joyful time which saw Cardinal Suenens concelebrating mass with almost 700 priests in St. Peter's basilica, it was also a period of tempering aspirations and a time to begin consolidating the faithful.

Prophecy: The Consolidation Phase

The following prophecy came out of the 1975 convention:

> Because I love you, I want to show you what I am doing in the world today. I want to prepare you for what is to come. Days of darkness are coming on the world, days of tribulation . . . Buildings that are now standing will not be standing. Supports that are there for my people will not be there. I want you to be prepared, my people, to know only me and to cleave to me and to have me in a way deeper than ever before. I will lead you into the desert . . . I will strip you of everything that you are depending on now, so you depend just on me. A time of darkness is coming on the world, but a time of glory is coming for my church, a time of glory is coming for my people. I will pour out on you all the gifts of my Spirit. I will prepare you for spiritual combat; I will prepare you for a time of evangelism that the world has never seen . . . And when you have nothing but me, you will have everything (*New Covenant*, July 1975:26).

Again we think it is significant that of all the prophecies and messages originating out of the 1975 International Conference, the one cited above and some with similar contents were viewed as important enough to reproduce and to discuss a number of times in subsequent issues of *New Covenant*. This theme of tribulation and disaster constituted the primary emphasis of the CCR from 1975 to the present. Even participants who returned from the 1977 National Conference on the Charismatic Renewal in the Catholic Church (which featured some 50,000 people from more than a dozen denominations) were talking about a mood of gloom and doom that hung over an otherwise exciting event. Perhaps gloom and doom understates the situation. Some of these prophetic messages speak of persecution, of the shedding of blood, and of the necessity for militant preparation to meet successfully these future challenges.

The important question asks why the emphasis changed from the triumphant one of 1974 to the pessimistic vision in 1975 and continued to the present. If we are correct in assuming that the events of 1975 were a significant letdown after the 1974 peaks and that the CCR leadership was beginning to perceive a stabilizing trend in movement growth, then we can perceive the value of a strategy that focuses on a number of external threats. Social science has long been aware that feelings of external threat tend to make the threatened group more cohesive (see chapter 3 for a more complete discussion of this point). If the CCR was not destined to attract increasing numbers of Roman Catholics, then one way to ensure that it simply does not die a quiet death, as it is absorbed into church routine, is to generate a sense of militancy in its members. The movement's fear of being absorbed, and thereby rendered virtually impotent, will be discussed at length in the next chapter.

These gloom and doom prophecies excited sufficient attention to warrant a special *New Covenant* article, "How should we respond? An interview with Kevin Ranaghan," (February 1978), designed to guide the concerned faithful.

Ranaghan affirms that these dismal prophecies have met the standard criteria for acceptable prophecies. He feels they are scripturally sound, that they have come from Christians whose lives are exemplary and whose past record on prophecy has been commendable, and that their basic content has been reiterated in different places at different times. When asked how individuals should respond to these prophecies, his answer reflects the argument previously presented:

> I think we have to realize that we're not, as individuals, in a position to deal with the collapse of, say, world-wide economic structures. But we are in a position to prepare ourselves. In these prophecies, the Lord consistently tells us to get our lives in good order, to grow in personal holiness, to strengthen our relationship with him. There is an urgent call to strengthen our relationships with other Christians. The Lord is warning

us because he wants us to begin preparations now, before the darkness is upon us (*New Covenant*, February 1978:13).

Ranaghan's advice to concerned charismatics is to become more intensely committed to movement goals and to surround themselves with close-knit circles of likeminded friends. It is a defensive posture, the circling of wagons to protect against the threats from without. It is a far cry from the expansiveness and optimism that characterized the mood of the CCR in 1974. It is a move designed to consolidate the faithful, not restore Christianity to the world. This defensive perspective was introduced almost solely via the mechanism of prophecy originating from the highest circles of CCR leadership. It thus appears to be an organizational directive designed to preserve a successful movement experiencing its first glimpse of what all movements must eventually face, dissolution and death. Further explanations of this stance will be offered in the next chapter.

Summary

In this chapter we have delineated the major types of impression management used by the CCR leadership to justify and legitimate their activities and organization. The leadership has demonstrated great talent in constructing definitions of reality that have appealed to a wide spectrum of both Catholics and non-Catholics, and have attracted the hierarchy and convinced many of them of the CCR's authentic prochurch orientation. These definitions have also guided members through the phases of movement flowering, growth, and recent stability. As in most things connected with the CCR, the leadership has acted with an uncommon working knowledge of human nature. However, even these talented individuals cannot meet all the exigencies necessary to preserve the movement within their desired goal structure. The mold of cooptation has already begun to collect on the fruit of the CCR. The shouts are turning to whispers, the exaltation and ecstasy to routine and drudgery. The eventual outcome of the CCR is our next subject.

7

The CCR and the Church:
Impact and Eventualities

We have consistently emphasized the generally amicable relationship existing between the CCR and its parent church. However, it is also true that the goals of the CCR founders present real problems for the church hierarchy. How is the movement's leadership to be reconciled with the existing leadership structures in the church? What is the future of charismatic communities? Does the call for more Christian communities, and the move toward a federation of these communities, predict an eventual confrontation with the church over matters of parish organization, liturgical forms, and related issues?

Also, while it is true that the CCR presents problems to the church, it is equally true that the church reaction to the CCR creates some obstacles to the achievement of the goals outlined by CCR founders. These points of interorganizational tension constitute the elements of this chapter. Once these points of tension are understood, we should be better able to assess the impact of the CCR on the church and to predict its future course.

CCR: A Cult, A Sect, Perhaps Neither

A question which inevitably arises in discussions of enthusiastic movements concerns their inherent potential for schism. Contemporary social science usually poses this question in terms of the venerable church-sect dichotomy of Troeltsch and Weber. Wilson (1959) views a sect as

> A voluntary association; membership is by proof to sect authorities of some claim to personal merit—such as knowledge of doctrine, affirmation of a conversion experience, or recommendation of members in good standing; exclusiveness is emphasized, and expulsion exercised against

those who contravene doctrinal, moral, or organizational precepts; its self-conception is of an elect, a gathered remnant, possessing special enlightenment; personal perfection is the expected standard of aspiration, in whatever terms this is judged; it accepts, at least as an ideal, the priesthood of all believers; there is a high level of lay participation; there is opportunity for the member spontaneously to express his commitment, the sect is hostile or indifferent to the secular order and to the state (p. 4).

Historically, some sects have become religious orders, such as the Franciscans and Dominicans, while others have left the parent church and eventually formed their own church structures. Fichter (1975) deals rather extensively with the question of whether the CCR can be viewed as a sect; he concludes that it more closely resembles a cult. A cult is a form of religious innovation that is primarily characterized by the intense involvement of the individual in some type of focused worship. Within the Catholic Church the passionate veneration of Mary could be viewed as a cultic practice. The cult poses no real threat to established authority.

While we certainly agree with much of Fichter's analysis, we do feel that his decision to characterize the CCR as a cult tends to avoid the real points of conflict existing between the CCR and the church. His analysis concentrates on the forms of involvement and commitment (the gifts of the spirit) and essentially neglects the demands for change within the church engendered by the goals of the CCR founders.

There can be little doubt that the CCR does have certain features that lead it to be characterized as a sect. The difficulties of trying to fit the model to actual cases, and the resulting proliferation of typologies resulting from such attempts, are adequately registered in the literature and need only a brief summary at this point.

Those who have worked within the framework of the church-sect typology have concentrated upon delineating the origin and characteristics of church and sect types. Some attention has been given to the explanatory utility of Troeltsch's work, for example, attempting to tie causally religious organizational types to particular ideological systems and their supporters.

Those focusing on origins have concentrated primarily on notions of social and personal deprivation. As we previously pointed out, many scholars have viewed sectarian membership and behavior as an outlet for those who have been frustrated in the socioeconomic order. After encountering sectlike groups that were not composed of the poor and wretched of the earth, scholars attempted to be consistent with deprivation ideas by positing some sort of personal or relative deprivation ("A negative discrepancy between legitimate expectations and actuality"—

Aberle, 1965:538). The CCR has not entirely escaped this type of analysis. In an unpublished paper, a cleric-scholar involved with the early Notre Dame community posits "affective deprivation" as a factor attracting people to the CCR. He notes that some people coming to the community "often feel very anxious, tense or guilty," but that the acceptance, affection, and sincerity of CCR members relieves these problems. In chapter 2 we argued against such monocausal explanations; we would simply add here that it is highly likely that some portion of the population attracted to any social activity—whether it be the Elks Club, "swinging marriages," or the P.T.A.—can be characterized as feeling "very anxious, tense or guilty." In all such analyses one fact seems evident: little attention is paid to the possibility that there may be positive motivation for joining a new religious movement. Our data and observations, as well as those of others (Hine, 1974; Gerlach, 1974), suggest that most people join the CCR because it provides a unique and powerful vehicle for expressing a faith commitment, and because its relationships and rituals extend perceptions of control over both the external and internal environment.

The interest in depicting church types and sect types in terms of characteristics has generated attempts ranging all the way from Pope's (1942) development of 21 features to Johnson's use of only a single characteristic. Out of this continuing debate over which characteristics are typical of sects grew the need to classify types of sects (Wilson, 1959) or other varieties of religious organizations, such as the denomination (Niebuhr, 1929; Becker, 1932) or the established sect (Yinger, 1970). All such efforts point to the recognition that the diversity of religious organizations is such that no single listing of characteristics, no matter how extensive, will conceptually cover all the empirical cases.

After more than half a century since Troeltsch's original formulation, sociologists of religion have—almost reluctantly, it seems—come to the point where at least some call for an end to efforts to further refine the typology. Demerath (1967) argues that the typology, for all its utility, should be abandoned in favor of concepts which apply "across the institutional spectrum." Such an approach has been attempted by Demerath and Hammond (1969) and Benson and Dorsett (1971). The latter pair attempted to develop a theory of religious organization employing the familiar concepts of bureaucracy, professionalization, secularization, and integration. It is our judgment that fruitful insights into understanding the nature of variation in religious organizations can best be served by linking religious organizations into the general framework or organizational theory. But where church-sect ideas provide valuable insights into the CCR, we will not hesitate to draw upon this literature. The CCR does contain features that have led to full-blown protests against established religious officialdom and the eventual formation of separatist groups. Whether or not this is a likely outcome for the entire CCR is a question we will treat in detail later.

Church Goals and CCR Goals

In the previous chapter we outlined the prodigious process through which CCR leadership ingratiated itself with the parent church. However, these efforts toward acceptance and harmony should not disguise the intention of the CCR to introduce serious modifications in church practices. In fact, the struggle for legitimacy and recognition appears to be part of the larger goal of bringing about meaningful change as painlessly as possible.

Spokespersons for the CCR generally affirm that the renewal did not originate by the adoption of any formal goals; yet it is clear that the structures which eventually emerged were very much the product of the original Notre Dame cadre led by Clark, Martin, and a handful of others. In order to evaluate more accurately what has happened in the CCR from 1967 to 1978, and to make a reasonable prediction of where it is headed, we now will compare the goals of the CCR with the goals of the parent church. This discussion is especially pertinent given the CCR leadership's ongoing attempts to define its goals as consonant with church history. Also this discussion will point out that the CCR is or is becoming at least two rather distinct organizations. It would indeed be presumptuous of us to try to do more than briefly outline the purposes which the Roman Catholic Church sees itself as fulfilling. Since the church is not completely uniform in its structure, numerous goals can be and have been attributed to it. Theologians, especially since Vatican II, have felt compelled to try to define the church's purposes. One noteworthy effort in this regard is provided by Dulles (1974), who discusses five models of the church from a historical perspective.

In Dulles's first model, the church is viewed as an Institution which "teaches, sanctifies, and commands, in each case identifying the church itself with the governing body or hierarchy" (p. 34). The goal of the church as institution is to provide eternal life for its members. For those outside the church, "it seeks to save their souls by bringing them into the institution." This model of the church is an ancient one and prevailed until about 1940.

The second model views the church as a Mystical Communion. Pius XII linked the mystical Body of Christ with the Roman Catholic Church. The goal of the mystical communion "is a spiritual or supernatural one. The Church aims to lead men into communion with the divine. . . . Wherever men are in the Church they have partly fulfilled the aim of their existence; they are, at least inchoatively, in union with God" (p. 54).

In the third model the church is seen as Sacrament. A sacrament is a sign of grace and the church of course is viewed as the sacrament of God which contains the grace signified in Christ. Its goal is "to purify and intensify men's response to the grace of Christ" so that they "become living symbols of divine love and beacons of hope in the world" (p. 67).

The fourth model of the church is that of a Herald. In this model the word is given primacy over the sacrament: "The Church is a herald—one who receives an official message with the commission to pass it on." Its goal is "simply to herald the message" (p. 78).

The final model offered by Dulles views the church as Servant. This theme, Dulles notes, has been pronounced in Catholic theology since Vatican II. Here the church is seen as a "man for others" (a model prominent in Protestant theology also). The goal of the servant church "is not primarily to gain new recruits for its own ranks, but rather to be of help to all men, wherever they are" (p. 91).

Dulles points out that these models are not independent of one another, and that problems result when a given group in the church seeks to impose a particular model upon all members. He does argue, however, that democratic processes at work in the western world suggest that the institutional model is no longer applicable to the situation in which the church finds itself today. The servant model has great appeal to many in the church today, but it is by no means as universally accepted as the one which the church should embrace. How to reconcile these various views of the church is a major task facing post-Vatican II Roman Catholicism; this task partially explains the contribution the CCR feels it is making in doing just this.

Goal Specification in the Charismatic Renewal Movement

How do the goals of the CCR correspond to those outlined by Dulles for the church at large? Does the CCR perceive itself as assisting Mother Church in reaching its goals, or has it set up a new agenda for both itself and the church to pursue? The answers to these questions help to explain the emerging structure of the CCR, and, at the same time, illuminate the conflicts and tensions existing between the hierarchy of the church and the leadership of the CCR.

O'Connor states that "the very point of this movement is the personal intervention of God in the lives of his people" (1971:29). Such a statement of purpose may seem to be of sufficient diffuseness to cover any legitimate undertaking; however, additional clues to the purposes of the CCR suggest that evangelism is the focus of its activities. God will intervene in the lives of his people when they are made aware of the message of the gospel—the call to commitment to Jesus Christ as savior. The message is one of "repentance, of faith, of baptism, of the gift of the Spirit." (Martin, 1971:59). This interpretation is supported by the theme of the 1978 National Conference on the Charismatic Renewal held at Notre Dame, Indiana. Kevin Ranaghan (quoted in Blattner, 1979) announced this theme: "I believe this conference marks the threshold of a major effort at mass evangelism, not only in the Catholic Charismatic Renewal, but in the entire Roman Catholic Church." The preaching of this message is one goal of the CCR, and it coincides with the third model presented by Dulles, the church as herald. It may seem, therefore, that a prominent view of the church as outlined by one of its leading scholars is congruous with the view of the CCR leadership. This is not necessarily the case, however. In specifying its goals, the CCR is calling for what it perceives to be a new image of the church. Proclamation of the Gospel may have always been accepted as a major function of the church, but it is the judgment of the CCR that the church has failed to direct its energies toward accomplishing this goal. It has experienced what is known as goal displacement in large organizations.

Goal displacement describes the not uncommon process whereby organizations devoted to the pursuit of given goals come to substitute goals other than those originally agreed upon as primary. The process occurs in all types of organizations, including religious ones. It occurs when "the actual activities of the organization become centered around the proper functioning of organizational procedures, rather than the achievement of the initial goals" (Sills, 1970:227). While there are several reasons for goal displacement in large organizations, a primary reason is that the employee's "interest in the ultimate purpose of the organization, in the 'common good,' becomes subordinate to his preoccupation with the problems involved in the maintenance of his post" (Selznick, 1943:52). The growth of the Salvation Army in Canada illustrates what the CCR feels has happened to the Roman Catholic Church (S.D. Clark, 1948). Initially devoted to evangelizing social outcasts, the Army devoted its primary energies to street preaching and revivals in Army barracks, where the poor, unaccustomed to churchgoing, might feel at home. In this direct appeal to those outside the established churches the Army was highly successful. Eventually, however, the Army felt the need to establish itself securely as an ongoing organization; therefore, it limited its work of evangelism and concentrated upon institutionalization. The decision "reflected the viewpoint of a leadership concerned with problems of administration and finance in opposition to the viewpoint of the evangelist, concerned only with saving souls" (S.D. Clark, 1948:426). Greater attention was paid to the educational and social position of those recruited into the Army's office ranks. A professsional ministry developed, and the Army became another institution devoted to maintaining its organizational strength at the expense of its former reclamation of the social outcasts of Canada.

Predictably, this development toward institutionalization in the Salvation Army led to protests and internal conflict within the Army. Defections occurred, and independent armies grew up under the leadership of those who had been officers in the Army. The protest movements emphasized the original goal of the Army, evangelism. The split within the Army resulted in a change in its nature and purpose, so that in the end it became a social welfare organization devoted only in part to its initial goal.

Is goal displacement characteristic of the Roman Catholic Church today? Martin and others in the CCR would argue that this is indeed the case. The renewal of the church, according to Martin, has failed because the church has "sacramentalized" but not "effectively evangelized" its members. The church has "presupposed" that its members are evangelized and committed to the person of Christ as Savior. But the evidence is contrary to this:

> Years of concentration on the important but secondary areas of the social implications of Christianity and structural reform, coupled with the almost total ignoring of what is truly fundamental to the Christian life, has produced in the lives of many a distorted vision and practice of Christianity which on many points are explicitly hostile to the foundation of the Christian life (R. Martin, 1971:13).

In a more recent critique of the Catholic Church, the National Service Committee of the CCR reiterates some of the arguments presented by Martin and goes on to detail others. In a document entitled "The State of the Catholic Church" (*New Covenant*, January 1978), this committee, while acknowledging strengths in the church, focuses on the following weaknesses: First, the church has not effectively developed true conversion or faith commitments in its members—the term "baptized pagans" is used to characterize the bulk of church members. Second, Catholic experience is one of individual struggle minus the support of a true community; the institutional church has failed in its attempts to generate a sense of community. Third, the church has not provided effective, scripturally based teaching to combat the deterioration of family life. Fourth, church leadership has been overly influenced by secular knowledge and has thereby become ineffectual. Leadership must be granted to those, both lay and cleric, who are truly committed to a scripturally based church. Finally, modern theology has capitulated to secular theories of human behavior and functioning and has lost the vision provided by Scripture. This capitulation to secular theory has resulted in a powerless and error-filled theology. The title of this article reflects the power the CCR leaders impute to their organization. The fact that the CCR feels capable of presenting a "State of the Church" document implies reams about felt autonomy and strength.

There can be little doubt that the CCR leadership views the modern church as beset by the problem of goal displacement. For the CCR, the renewal of the church must begin with a recognition that "the work of evangelism . . . is clearly the primary mission of the Church" (R. Martin, 1971:39). Such an affirmation from a practicing Catholic may strike the impartial observer as somewhat ironic. Has not the church always perceived itself as having a mission of evangelizing the world? Has not the church always called upon its members to lead spirit-filled lives? The answer, of course, is "yes"; and in stressing this fact the CCR seeks to relate its activities to the rich tradition of the church. There is, however, a significant difference in the stress the CCR puts upon individual personal renewal and that which is traditionally embraced by the church. CCR members view the condition of being baptized in the spirit as a normative expectation on the part of all. In answer to the question "do you think the gifts of the Spirit referred to by Paul (1 Corinthians 12) are for EVERYONE?" 91 percent of our respondents said "yes."

If the goal of the CCR is to increase significantly the number of committed, spirit-filled Christians, there must be some specific means through which this kind of renewal can occur. Although the prayer group is the dominant social expression of the CCR, it is definitely *not* the prayer group that Clark, Martin, and some other CCR leaders view as the means to create a true renewal.

Christian Communities: Havens in a Hostile World

There has never been any doubt that the establishment of Christian communities has been viewed by the Ann Arbor-South Bend leadership as the primary vehicle through which meaningful change in church structure is to be generated. A move toward geographically defined communities of Catholic Charismatics can best be understood in terms of whether the CCR views itself as a reform movement, which seeks to make radical changes, or a renewal movement, which attempts to reemphasize orthodoxy. Both of these terms are used, sometimes interchangeably, by different Charismatics, which indicates some lack of consensus within the CCR as to how far it is prepared to push for the establishment of truly separate communities with relatively autonomous leadership cadres. It is possible that some Charismatics may eventually withdraw and establish communities that no longer relate to the church. History provides ample evidence of such possibilities. Daniel Bell (1971:487) observes that if one is to provide a base for acting out certain religious experiences, then it becomes necessary to create a "continuing community," which is able to provide a "continuing system of transcendental meaning."

> In a religious culture, the symbols are everywhere and pervade the daily life without notice. Today the religious impulse and emotion may be present, but they lack the anchorage of a grounded culture, and are thus necessarily compartmentalized, existing only in the form of specialized experiences in isolated theaters or churches. However heightened such expressions may be, they remain fragmented moments.

Vividly aware of the condition described by Bell, Catholic Charismatics believe that a possible solution to the problem in a nonreligious culture is to create a new environment in which the symbols will be "everywhere." Father Avery Dulles comments upon this possibility (1974:17):

> Charismatically-gifted persons could easily fall into the trap of withdrawing from the general life of their own church and be tempted to set up, for all practical purposes, their own hierarchy of lay authorities, their own liturgy of prayer and proclamation, their own norms of Christian conduct and even, to some extent, their own doctrinal standards.

While some students of the movement stress the fact that the movement is currently within the church, such a view tends to neglect the prominent position advocated by CCR leaders such as Clark, Martin, and others that the CCR must move in the direction of Christian communities. Since this view is so salient in Clark's writings, a brief summary and analysis of his position will be particularly helpful in understanding exactly what is being proposed as a Christian community by Catholic Charismatics.

While Clark does not offer a how-to manual for the creation of proposed Christian communities, he did disseminate an unpublished document, "The Covenant of a Brotherhood," which clearly outlines his vision of a somewhat ideal community. Our copy of "The Covenant of a Brotherhood" was passed on to us by a former member of the True House community at Notre Dame. It reportedly came from Ann Arbor and was written by Steve Clark in the spring of 1973.

In a section entitled "Basics," Clark sets the goal of the movement as one of knowing God fully, committing oneself completely to the Lord, and of committing one's loyalty to the renewal of the church. The way of life is defined as a brotherhood of mutual support and encouragement, a total commitment of one's life throughout the entirety of one's life. Also, voluntary self-denial is considered a necessity in order to maintain individual commitment.

In a second section, "Personal Relations," Clark develops a topic that is frequent in his writing: the techniques of providing intense, lasting personal relationships. All "signs of possessiveness, exclusiveness, jealousy, and an anxiousness to please the other or to be with the other" must be avoided. Open affection, obedience and submission, teaching and admonishing, support and encouragement are to characterize these relationships. "Brothers" are to share every aspect of their lives with one another and avoid erotic entaglements or relationships that could lead toward marriage. Parents should be honored, but family commitments are not one's primary obligation.

A section entitled "Possessions" advocates austerity, common finances, and simplicity in all aspects of life. Members are informed that they "can keep a library of books that are useful for spiritual reading, for teaching Christianity, and for knowing better how to perform the service the Lord has given us." Members will also regularly examine personal possessions and give away unnecessary items.

The fourth major heading, "Order," outlines authority relationships in the brotherhood. All authority resides in the head, who is to be willingly obeyed and kept informed of the consequences of his decisions. However, the head is enjoined to also seek advice from the brothers, and brothers are to be active participants in the decision making process. Decisions are reached "by coming to a oneness of mind about what the Lord wants."

The section "Daily Life" advocates personal and shared prayer, regular times of sharing, and a common main meal. Sharing life's events, showing affection and positive attitudes, and avoiding negative symbolism are all stressed. Life is to involve systematic self-denial. Brothers can live "in the world" as long as their ideals are not compromised. Guests are to be cared for and welcomed.

The remainder of the document discusses "Our Commitment as a Brotherhood." This section generally elaborates many of the points made previously. The commitment is considered a lifetime one, and the participant is to be protected against outside influence. The following sections illustrate these points:

> We therefore commit ourselves for the rest of our lives to have and to use as little as possible, never to marry, and to live a common life with brothers who are committed to the same ideal.

> We can send a brother to another brotherhood if he agrees to go or the head can give permission for a brother to transfer to another brotherhood

upon the request of that brother. No one, however, should leave our brotherhood unless he will become part of a brotherhood in which the commitments he made for the rest of his life will be safeguarded.

When we joined the brotherhood, we left our parents' household. Our primary commitment is to the life together of our brothers. All responsibility for our welfare belongs to our brothers and no longer to our families.

Whenever possible, no one of us will make trips or go to conference or on visits that keep him away from home without having a partner go with him. The partners will pray together, share together what they are doing, and talk over what they plan to do. If possible they should talk together three times a day and sleep in the same house at night.

What Clark has outlined in "The Covenant of a Brotherhood" is an all-encompassing system of social control not unlike the medieval monastic orders. The primary difference is that members need not share the same dwelling nor the same geographical space. It is essentially a monastic system adopted to the exigencies of urban life.

Whenever possible, we will live together in a house or houses of the brotherhood in which the covenant is followed.

For reasons of service or of helping others experience a life like ours, some of us can live with others who do not belong to the brotherhood.

It will be possible for groups of us to live in other cities and still be part of the brotherhood.

The problem with Clark's vision of a brotherhood is that it could hardly hope to attract more than a handful of zealots who share his faith commitment. This is especially true concerning the injunction against marriage, even though Clark and several others have taken vows of celibacy. The remainder of the document fairly well describes the structure of most Charismatic communities. The Ann Arbor community, begun by Clark, Martin, and a few others, has been the model for others who would construct a Christian community.

Clark's wider vision of church renewal is presented in his books *Building Christian Communities* (1972) and *Unordained Elders and Renewal Communities* (1975). Possessing a sensitive view of humankind's social nature, he argues that if one is to live in the twentieth century as a Christian, then he must be sustained by a social-cultural milieu that has its roots in Christian philosophy with accompanying ethics and normative guidelines. He judges the present milieu deficient in this manner and largely incapable of being converted to such an environment. Such a view is shared by many sociologists of religion, particularly Peter Berger.

Berger (1967) argues that the relatively monolithic world view of the medieval ages in which church and society worked to complement each other was "lost, probably irretrievably, upon its dissolution at the beginning of the modern ages." The modern age has been characterized by many as a secular era and, while the complexities of this definition are beyond the scope of this discussion, few serious scholars disagree with the basic assumption that the advent of a technological society dramatically reduced the possibility that human beings could any longer define their life perspective primarily from the Judaeo-Chrisitian point of view. If secularization is one of the defining motifs in contemporary society, then the individual who wishes to live his or her life in total conformity with the Christian philosophy does face extreme obstacles in the way of achieving that goal.

One way to provide Christians with a hospitable environment in which to practice their faith would be to restructure society. Clark, with an insight not common among fervent reformers, recognizes that "the approach of making society as a whole Christian does not seem very feasible, because society as a whole is resistant to Christianity" (Clark, 1972:45). Thus Clark opts for the abandonment of the local diocese as the focal point of community, since "it cannot meet the daily needs of Christian people" and chooses to "create something that is not there now—a community" (S.B. Clark, 1972a:82–83).

Clark suggests the following options for consideration by would-be community builders. First, he cautions *against* a mere restructuring of existing parish lines by subdividing them into smaller units. Neither dioceses nor the congregation have the ability to function like true Christian communities. A second approach would be to "raise a flag outside the present parochial system, take the people who rally round and form them into a community" (Clark, 1972:83). Even though he feels this approach has much to recommend it, he recognizes the probable consequence of losing touch with many people with whom the parish even today has contact. His third and favored approach is to encourage the formation of several communities of people who are presently within the parish structure. These different communities would still meet on Sundays to celebrate "*their* community's liturgy" (S.B. Clark, 1972:84—emphasis added).

It is clear that Clark's recommendations, if enacted, would call for a major restructuring of the present parish organization in the Roman Catholic Church. In the restructuring of any existing organizational form a central question emerges: Who will provide leadership for the new configuration? Will existing leadership be replaced entirely? Will efforts be made to retrain former leaders to assume new roles and new duties? Obviously those presently in authority will not look favorably upon their replacement by others. They may, it can be anticipated, strenuously resist retraining. Clark addresses this issue forthrightly and with no effort to bypass the consequences for the parish priest, bishop, or other memebers of the Catholic hierarchy. He calls for a serious reconsideration of the present means whereby Catholic priests are trained and then assigned to serve the local parish. Effective pastoral care is not ensured by modern seminary training, which, in fact, mirrors all of the problems associated with the rest of secular society. "The seminary approach is not only inadequate as a way of selecting priests, it is also inadequate as a process of formation" (S.B. Clark, 1972a:141).

Clark's vision of effective pastoral care ties in with the authority structure exhibited by the Ann Arbor community. Effective leadership is that which has demonstrated an ability to commit others to Christ. Clark uses the term "natural leaders." Also, effective pastoral care is built around a model of service to the religious community. This type of service is not seen primarily as administrative and bureaucratic, but as one of complete self-absorption and self-immolation for the enhancement of a true community of believers. Clark is very straightforward in suggesting the direction the church should take in seeking effective leadership: "Ordination in the Church will be most effective when those who are ordained are the natural leaders of the Christian people" (S.B. Clark, 1972a:141).

Those persons in the CCR who share Clark's emphasis on Christian communities are advocates of significant change in existing church structure. The justification for this thrust toward new leadership structures is found in the documents of Vatican II, which stressed a greater democratization of power in the church. The relatively recent revival of the diaconate has been one official response to the shared authority emphasis of Vatican II. In fact, some prominent CCR leaders have been made deacons and are involved in deacon-training programs in the United States. However, the expansion of the diaconate would not completely meet the goals of the communitarian wing of the CCR.

The intriguing drama of Roman Catholics speaking in tongues, prophesying, faith healing, and controlling people's lives in monklike communities has tended to cover the CCR with a media fog, so that its primary goals are often obscure to the casual observer. The communitarian wing of the CCR appears to be a true renewal or even restoration movement, in the sense that the ultimate goal is the full commitment of individuals to an apostolic or at least an ideal of an apostolic Christianity. The issue is the effective initiation of individuals into a Biblical Christianity, so that the secularization of the modern church can be halted, or even reversed. A document entitled "A Statement of the Theological Basis of the Catholic Charismatic Renewal" makes this point unambiguously:

> One can only be a Christian by personal commitment. Each adult must say *yes* to the baptism received as an infant. . . . If one were to point to the strengths of the renewal, one would mention the genuine conversion experience which leads to a living faith, a profound love of the Eucharist, a new appreciation for the sacrament of penance, healing of interpersonal relationships, ·moral transformation, renewed sense of discipleship, awareness of the necessity of firm doctrinal basis, fidelity to the bishop and the Pope (*New Covenant*, January 1974).

Thus the hoopla surrounding tongue speaking and the dramatic gifts misses the target. The communitarian wing of the CCR does not really need these gifts if alternative methods of committing the faithful can be found. An all-enveloping community is just such a structure. The older religious orders fostered total commitment through the social control mechanisms of tight-knit communities, intense prayer, public confessions, fasting, and meditation. Although glossolalic utterances have been noted in the prayer life of the ancients, and some prophesying and healing did occur, these certainly were not the predominant form of life, nor were they particularly stressed. As we argued in chapter 5, the "gifts" are excellent commitment devices, and hence are only one means of achieving the goal of highly committed Christians.

This interpretation is strongly reinforced by Clark's own writings. In *Building Christian Communities* Clark mentions the Cursillo movement much more frequently than he does the CCR. The reason is quite simple and relates to our discussion in chapter 4: the Cursillo movement taught Clark and others the basic techniques of influencing people. Clark tells us that "a certain kind of group dynamics was learned from the Cursillo movement and is now used broadly throughout the Church outside the Cursillo movement" (Clark, 1972:161). In an article entitled "Authority in Christian Communities," Clark often uses the language of the Cursillo to refer to relationships between a master and disciple in a Christian community (*New Covenant*, December 1975). The term "to be formed," or the word "formation," is very much a Cursillo term and reflects the goals of both the Cursillo and the communitarian wing of the CCR. As we argued in chapter 4, the CCR is in one sense an extension of the Cursillo movement. Both involve very tight systems of social control, the major difference being that the CCR has more portable and widely attractive commitment techniques.

Again, Clark's own writings are straightforward testimonies to the fact that it is not the CCR per se that he is devoted to but the goal of intensely committing people to an idealized biblical form of Christianity. Clark is apparently quite willing to support any set of activities which serve this end: "The more the developments of modern society make people less and less satisfied with performing formal worship out of duty, the more the Church needs movements which lead people to a spontaneous, freely chosen worship" (Clark, 1972a:158–159). Note that Clark refers to movements in general and not to the CCR specifically.

To the extent that CCR leaders share Clark's vision, the goals of the CCR present some real problems for the traditional parish structure of the church. Clark offers his type of Christian community as a viable alternative to the traditional parish structure. One is immediately faced, however, with the reality of the CCR. Approximately 96 percent of the renewal consists of prayer groups—most of which have some kind of parish contact—and the vast majority of these people would never seriously consider abandoning their present life styles for the total environment of the Christian community. All of this simply means that the goals of the CCR founding fathers are not and cannot be the goals of the vast bulk of its membership.

This source of tension within the CCR has been noted by other observers, including some of its own leadership:

> There are two streams within the Catholic Charismatic renewal: the prayer groups, large and small, and the covenant communities. . . . Because the covenant communities have tighter bonds than the prayer groups, arising out of mutual submission of the central teams, they form groups of unusual strength. In discipline, formation, pastoral care, personnel, and financing, they have resources far *beyond* what the ordinary prayer group can hope to attain (McDonnell, 1978:23).

McDonnell further notes that communities are forming national and international federations, and that the larger, more powerful covenanted communities set national and regional policies that affect those in the prayer groups.

Clerical Influx into the CCR

An important and related development has been the continuing clericalization of the CCR. Each year since the 1967 beginning at Duquesne University has witnessed more and more priests become charismatics, taking over leadership of prayer groups, and appearing on CCR leadership committees. McDonnell cogently describes part of the problem that continued clericalization creates for the CCR: "The covenant communities are mostly lay in membership. Priests who are involved in the renewal tend to identify with prayer groups and are interested in parish renewal. The priest is trained to think in terms of the parish" (McDonnell, 1978:25).

What this amounts to is essentially an identity crisis for the CCR. What began as a grand experiment in working toward new structures of lay leadership designed to increase member commitment to Biblical discipleship now faces the danger of being quietly coopted into the existing parish structures under the guidance of well-intentioned parish priests, many of whom are themselves Charismatics. The danger is that what will remain of the CCR is the form and not the substance. The prayer meeting, with its tongue speaking, prophesying, and testifying, becomes something akin to traditional rosary devotions or stations-of-the-cross devotions. The few who are interested will attend, acknowledge the leadership of the local cleric, and participate in a relatively highly stylized ritual; and all that will be added to the parent church is another weekly meeting that has little or no impact on the larger structure. McDonnell apparently recognizes the dangers outlined in the above paragraph, for he tells us that "It will be a sad day for both the renewal and the Church if it [the movement] becomes clericalized."

It is quite evident that CCR leadership has undergone a significant transformation since its early years. An examination of changing faces in the National Service Committee will illustrate the point. The National Service Committee, officially born in 1970, is the group primarily responsible for organizing the national conferences and leadership meetings, for publishing *New Covenant* magazine, and for controlling the Communication Center, which sells tapes and literature judged pertinent to movement goals. In recent years an advisory committee, composed of a wider spectrum of national leaders, has been added and meets with the National Service Committee to offer advice and to receive guidance in terms of desirable operating goals.

The initial National Service Committee (1970) was simply a codification of the dominant leadership in the CCR at that time. It was composed almost exclusively of men who had known each other during those early days at Notre Dame: James Byrne, Father Edward O'Connor, Kevin Ranaghan, Steve Clark, Ralph Martin, Bert Ghezzi, and Father George Kosicki. Most of these men have had rather extensive contact with and involvement in influential Christian communities. The five laypersons on the 1970 National Service Committee were, before 1973, something of a Who's Who in Catholic Charismatic community circles. Byrne was the head of the now defunct True House community at Notre Dame; Ranaghan became one of the principal organizers of the People of Praise community in South Bend, Indiana; Clark and Martin were the founders and heads of the Ann Arbor Word of God community (Clark still heads that community though he works in Belgium); Ghezzi played a prominent role in community building in Grand Haven, Michigan, and then went to the Ann Arbor community and replaced Ralph Martin as editor of *New Covenant*. During this time clerics made up a mere 29 percent of the National Service Committee. One of these, Father Edward O'Connor, was never a major figure in the CCR, and eventually resigned from the National Service Committee after some discontent with the Clark-Martin policies.

In 1973 all of the original Service Committee members remained, with the exception of Father O'Connor and James Byrne (who left the CCR after the True House scandals in 1973). Now, however, three more clerics were added, including Bishop Joseph McKinney of Grand Rapids, Michigan. McKinney, himself a Charismatic, has been a bulwark for conventional hierarchical church authority within the CCR. He has consistently stressed the need for priests to shepherd the CCR in order to help prevent abuses and excesses. In addition to those mentioned above, Paul deCelles, another leader of the South Bend People of Praise, was added to the National Service Committee. The National Service Committee was, in 1973, 44 percent clerics.

By 1976 Martin and Ghezzi were no longer part of the National Service Committee. Martin had moved with Steve Clark to Belgium to help Cardinal Suenens with the international aspects of the CCR. That year four more priests were added to the National Service Committee (a priest and a layperson were dropped from the 1973 list) along with two prominant laypersons. The N.S.C. reached a peak of clerical involvement in 1976, when 63 percent of their membership were clerics. In 1978 the percentage of clerics dropped to 55 percent and the first two women to ever serve on the National Service Committee were added. The addition of women to the N.S.C. was probably a result of the on-going criticism that the CCR was sexist. The most vocal critic in this regard was J. Massyngberde Ford, professor of theology at Notre Dame. By 1978 only one of the original 1970 group remained—Kevin Ranaghan of the People of Praise in South Bend.

There are other indications that the communitarian, Clark-Martin wing of the CCR is losing influence and that the cleric-led parish groups are gaining influence in the CCR. In March of 1976, the Paulist Press began publishing a new magazine called the *Catholic Charismatic*. Its editor reports that the magazine was a result of a dream "of a new charismatic magazine with more breadth and depth in the Catholic tradition than was then available" (Lange, 1976:2). This editor was certainly aware of *New Covenant* and obviously viewed it as weak in its treatment of things traditionally Catholic. Table 3 presents the results of our own analysis of the content of 395 articles in 42 issues of *New Covenant*. Our conclusion was that *New Covenant* did indeed deal quite extensively with traditional Catholic religious issues. This is especially true in recent years. This makes it all the more interesting that a new

Table 3 Content of Randomly Selected Issues of *New Covenant* magazine between 1972 and 1978.

Content	1972–73	1974–75	1976–78
1. The "gifts" and charismatic religious practices	16%	20%	8%
2. Mechanics of prayer meetings and community construction	7%	7%	5%
3. General religious themes likely to be heard in any Sunday Catholic homily	8%	14%	29%
4. Social action	21%	3%	1%
5. Movement progress	12%	15%	9%
6. Testimonies	11%	15%	13%
7. Christian family, youth, and personal relationships	3%	4%	18%
8. Ecumenicism	1%	6%	6%
9. Charismatic activity in other churches	1%	5%	5%
10. International aspects of the CCR	9%	4%	5%
11. Other	11%	7%	1%
	100%	100%	100%
	N=76	N=165	N=154

Total N=395 Articles
42 Issues

magazine had to be founded in order to adequately cover "Catholic" issues.

The editor of the *Catholic Charismatic* further tells us that after a good deal of meeting and discussing, the decision was made to "explore the best that is Catholic, that is, discover and share the way the Spirit has been and is working in the long history of the Church and throughout the breadth of it." Again the decision to publish *Catholic Charismatic* must reflect the judgment of its founders that *New Covenant*, the publication of the CCR founders, is somehow deficient in its treatment of Catholic issues. The authors of *Catholic Charismatic* also refer to the "first generation" of relevant literature. If the *Catholic Charismatic* is any reflection of the second generation of authors, then it becomes obvious that the second generation is disproportionately clerical in nature. This is especially true of the editorial staff of *Catholic Charismatic*, which is over 75 percent cleric.

We believe that the growing involvement (usually in some leadership capacity) of priests in prayer groups, the clericalization of the National Service Committee, and the creation and publication of the *Catholic Charismatic* all reflect the general clericalization of the CCR. While the clericalization of the movement need not be inherently negative, it must be viewed as the effective termination of the goals of the CCR founders. A movement dominated by clerics is not likely to produce a viable, extensive cadre of lay leaders, nor promote the building of more covenant communities. Whatever form of lay leadership, if any, that emerges from such an organization will still be controlled by the traditional hierarchy and reflect the hierarchy's interests. A movement dominated by clerics cannot produce the radical structural change envisioned by Clark as essential for the survival of a vibrant Christianity in a secular era.

The CCR and the Emergence of Communes in the United States

Besides the growing clericalization of the CCR, there are other forces mitigating against the realization of the communitarian's goals. It is very likely that the principal communitarian drive of the CCR has all but ground to a halt in the United States. It must be remembered that the growth period of the CCR communities paralleled the boom period of the more general commune movement in the United States. Hugh Gardner (1978) discusses the period betwen 1965 and 1973 as that time in American history that witnessed the emergence of both rural and urban communes at a rate that dwarfed anything similar during the previous 200 years. He also ties that emergence of the commune movement to prosperity and to the feeling of many youths that America had become "a complete social, political, cultural, moral, and ecological wasteland" (1978:4). Gardner also sees a search for transcendence in the drug culture that was an integral part of the modern commune movement. Like the CCR communards, their secular counterparts "were white, came from middle-class and professional homes, had been to college and often held advanced degrees, were twenty to thirty years old, . . . and had been at least peripherally involved in the protest politics of the time" (1978:240). Gardner also suggests that many of the secular communards were users of psychedelic drugs. While some CCR people have admitted to drug use prior to CCR involvement this is certainly not true of the bulk of its leadership or membership.

The point is that the CCR communitarian emphasis flourished, in part, because certain general societal conditions favored that form of social experimentation. The conditions promoting communal living seem to have all but vanished. In particular, the prosperity (or more importantly, the image of prosperity) of the mid to late 1960s is gone. The bulk of today's college students seem frighteningly pragmatic compared to their counterparts of a few years ago. Intense competition in the job market does not promote fantasies of radical experimentation with alternative life styles. We suggest that one of the reasons Steve Clark and Ralph Martin went to work in 1975 in Brussels on international aspects of the CCR was their realization that their goals for church renewal were not likely to be realized in the United States. However, cultural conditions in other countries may promote a more fertile soil for the building of Christian communities.

Parish Renewal and Sectarianism

All the above suggests that the CCR is not going to accomplish the radical structural change envisioned by its founders. In fact, there is growing dissension over what the primary goals of the CCR should be. A substantial part of the CCR wants to put issues of parish renewal ahead of the building of Christian communities. Ralph Martin (1978:21) addresses himself to this problem, and essentially admits that the CCR is a long way from effecting any substantial change in the church:

> The fact that there are relatively few parishes on the way to substantive renewal, and relatively few covenant communities, points to the intrinsic difficulty of such attempts. The fact that more than 95% of the charismatic renewal expresses itself in prayer groups of fewer than 50 people says something about the relative scarcity at this time of leadership resources necessary to move on to a deeper level.

However, in the extremely flexible leadership style that has characterized the CCR founders, Martin tells us that both parish renewal and community building are legitimate goals in certain circumstances, as long as the primary goal of renewing "corporate Christian life" is served. He goes on to warn against schism within the movement: "Renewal is difficult enough and the number of dedicated Christians working for it is so relatively small that we can hardly afford the obstacles caused by polarization over approaches" (1978:21).

It is still true, however, that there are a growing number of CCR spokespersons vigorously promoting parish renewal. George Martin (no relation to Ralph Martin), a lay traditionalist within the CCR, tells us that: "The goal of a charismatically renewed Catholic Church demands that the charismatic renewal become integrated into the life of the parish and bring renewal to the parish" (Martin, 1976:115). He presents a model of the "cheerful servant" as the way to effective parish renewal. If parish members who are also CCR participants immerse themselves vigorously and cheerfully in worthwhile parish activities, they will serve as models to those outside the CCR. The hope is that the "cheerful servants" can stimulate a general parish renewal.

One parish priest (cited in *New Covenant*, November 1976:21–23) who has apparently been instrumental in bringing about renewal in his own parish actually argues that there are some antithetical elements between notions of covenanted communities and renewed parishes:

> We focused our attention on serving the parish. We tried to support and strengthen all the existing services such as the Rosary and Altar Society. It was important that the people not feel deprived of these traditional parish functions just because our prayer group had arrived in their midst.
>
> Also, we eventually dropped both the community name, the Word of God, and the community covenant. You can't have a covenant community within a parish community—the community here and the parish there. The community appears to be an elitist group and that leads to division in the parish.

Randall is well aware that his charismatically renewed parish is unique. He acknowledges that parish renewal is not likely unless the local pastor is the head of the parish prayer group, which is extremely rare. Pastors have a vested interest in the traditional forms of worship and have little to gain by promoting prayer groups in their parishes; in fact, they risk a great deal by siding with what is usually a poorly understood and a somewhat extreme minority in the parish. It is unlikely that parish renewal along CCR lines will make headlines in the near future.

Is sectarianism, then, a likely possibility for the CCR? Exactly what will be the CCR's contribution to the church? Where is the CCR headed?

It should be obvious at this point that we do not view sectarianism as a likely outcome for the CCR. This is not to say that certain small groups within the CCR might not decide to proceed independently of constituted authority; indeed, some rather isolated instances of rejection of church authority by prayer groups have already taken place. We talked at length with one lay prayer leader who had driven away interested clerics and who had become, in effect, his prayer group's "pastor." He did all the preaching, teaching, and interpreting of Scripture. This type of leadership, however, is a rare event, involving only a handful of CCR leaders.

There remain some real differences between the various manifestations of the movement and the members' attitudes toward certain church-related issues and church authority. At one point in our statistical analysis, we divided our sample of prayer groups into those that had strong lay leadership, weak lay leadership, weak clerical leadership, and moderate-to-strong clerical leadership. "Strong" was conceptualized as being stable, effective in controlling meetings and inducing enthusiasm, and consensus among members that the leader (or leaders) was dynamic and "of the Lord." "Weak" was the relative absence of most or all of these characteristics. Those groups having strong lay leadership exhibited statistically significant differences from all other types of group in terms of allegiance to church authority and other church issues. Members of groups with strong lay leadership were likely to be much more antiauthority, much less enthusiastic about bringing veneration of the Virgin Mary into the movement, and much less aligned with church stands on birth control and priestly celibacy. (We omitted Protestants from this analysis.) On the other hand, members of groups having strong clerical leadership were much more likely to go along uncritically with church authority (both bishops and pastors), to welcome veneration of the Virgin Mary, and to mirror church stands on birth control and priestly celibacy. Groups with weak lay or clerical leadership were in between on all these issues.

The data discussed above seem to indicate that sectarianism is indeed a possible outcome for those groups having strong lay leadership. However, sectarianism is always the outcome of a relationship between the parent body and the world builders. It is quite possible that outright, blatant opposition from the church would stimulate a withdrawal reaction among those groups characterized by dynamic lay leadership and coalesce them into a true schismatic movement. However, the key to that eventuality is the nature of the church's reaction, and it is highly unlikely that the hierarchy will bring any kind of official, negative sanctions to bear against the CCR.

There are a number of reasons for this probability. The church, with an abundant history of experience in dealing with cult and sect groups, has amply demonstrated the ability to envelope dissenting groups with a mantle of loving acceptance, thereby keeping them in the fold and eliminating their destructive potential. Modern Christian churches can hardly afford to expel committed members at a time when the competition between Christian and other religious, and Christian and secular ideologies is so acute. The modern ecumenical movement must be viewed as a survival tactic of a threatened world view. Finally, the within-the-church rhetoric of the CCR is authentic. It would be extremely difficult for CCR leaders to reconcile separation with the decade of intense prochurch activity that has characterized the CCR literature and programs.

If schism is unlikely, what options remain? Can the CCR continue its past successes and eventually involve large numbers of Roman Catholics so that the movement goals of renewal can be realized? We guess this possibility has close to a zero probability of occurrence. We have already presented data demonstrating the leveling and decline of the rate of growth. National and international meetings are still well attended by enthusiastic participants, but the number of participants is not increasing, and the enthusiasm lacks the intensity that exploded in the 1974 National Convention at Notre Dame. Inevitable routinization is covering the CCR with a life-stifling mold. As we previously argued, recent prophecies emanating from the CCR leadership tell of times of trouble and challenge. The first blush of spring in 1967 through 1972 gave way to the glorious summer of 1972 to 1974, faded into the increasingly somber autumn of 1975 through 1978, and is likely to evolve into a very harsh winter.

This prediction does not mean, however, that the CCR will not continue to provide a meaningful faith commitment to individuals. It does mean that this experience is not likely to reach the large numbers of persons necessary for a meaningful renewal.

The most likely outcome of the CCR is a quiet, unceremonious absorption into the existing structure. Individuals will continue, though at a decreasing rate, to speak in tongues, prophesy, and occasionally heal; these activities, however, will eventually give way to a simple prayer service where highly committed, biblically oriented Catholics can mutually reinforce their commitment and world view. Prayer groups will continue to be islands of faith maintenance and mutual aid in a generally hostile social environment, but they will be, and already are, routinized and gently coopted by well-intentioned clerics and procleric laypersons.

It is also possible that the cooptation process will involve ordaining some of the more outstanding CCR leaders. This possibility is already under consideration with Steve Clark. Perhaps the more radical CCR leaders will eventually form one more religious order within the Catholic Church: in the church but not coextensive with it; in society but not of society.

The CCR has highlighted the fact that nominal Christianity is basically a capitulation to secular ideology. There appears to be increasing recognition among all the Christian churches that the equating of Christianity with secular humanism is tantamount to an admission that Christian culture has nothing distinctive to offer people. When Christian clerics are more embarrassed to mention God, sin, and resurrection than they are to discuss ego, id, and libido, they dramatically demonstrate their own aversion to anything distinctively Christian and their acceptance of secular religion with its panoply of gods, behavioral prescriptions, and cultish fads. The CCR, and other related trends in Christian circles, can be viewed as an effort to preserve at least some remnants of a culture. Whether these attempts have any possibility of success is the subject of our final chapter.

8
Waning of the CCR

It is axiomatic in social science to characterize periods of rapid social change as fountainheads of social movements. During such times some individuals perceive certain elements of the changing socio-cultural scene as serving their particular interest, and social movements arise which seek to accelerate aspects of that change. Other individuals perceive the changing socio-cultural patterns as threats to their values and lifestyles and seek to join with likeminded persons to retard the pace of change or to recapture valued aspects of the past. The CCR can be viewed more as a result of the retarding than of the accelerating process.

Actually the CCR was only part of a cultural pattern. During the time of its growth there was a resurgence of interest in ethnic roots. The popular assimilationist "melting pot" notion was increasingly challenged by an emphasis on pride in one's racial and ethnic differences. The concept of roots was manifested in a return, even if only a symbolic one, to the family, tribe, and church. Roy C. Buck has noted the nostalgic and romantic elements of tourism (1978), which increasingly appeal to those who seemingly prefer to look back rather than ahead.

When the Second Vatican Council opened the doors of the institutional church few observers could have accurately predicted which way the "winds of change" would blow. In the modernization of the liturgy much of what used to promote a sense of awe and mystery was eliminated. The Latin Mass was replaced by the vernacular, and many of the more grandiose aspects of traditional ritual were streamlined and simplified. Similarly, the traditional images of inviolable authority relations between layperson and clergy gave way to more collegial types of association. The laity were now encouraged to take a more active part in shaping the church, to move toward equality with those in positions of authority. While such democratization serves modern political values, it does not promote a sense of awe and respect of those in authority.

These kinds of dramatic changes encouraged experimentation by both clergy and laypeople, as they sought to redefine the social boundaries of a now ambiguous reality and to recapture a sense of transcendence that tends to promote intense commitment. Home masses and prayer groups of many varieties characterized the Post Vatican II milieu. Out of these churnings the CCR emerged, grew, and maintained itself as an effective organization at the fringes of the institutional church.

The characteristics that made the CCR successful have been discussed in detail: a talented leadership who understood the importance of effective organization, along with a preexisting network of relationships and communication channels. Moreover, of crucial significance was the discovery of techniques which promote feelings of awe and transcendence. The example of classical pentecostals (Knox, 1950) gave these seekers what they needed to build commitment and to attract others to their cause: the Gifts of the Spirit.

Among these Gifts of the Spirit, speaking in tongues, healing, and prophecy were particularly important. In each of these the sense of God using the individual as an agent inspired feelings of wonderment and power that would be difficult to capture in more conventional rituals or settings. The practice of these Gifts brought people together and encouraged a sense of community inspired by the perception that they were a "chosen people."

The early CCR fully expected to become a force which would set the floundering institutional church back on an "authentically" Christian path. Indeed, many of the experiences of those first few years promoted this expectation: membership roles increased significantly; the secular media and other religions took an intense interest in the movement; but, most importantly, the highest elements of the church hierarchy began to take the CCR seriously and apparently to encourage at least some of its activities.

However, this early optimism gave way to cautious pessimism as it became increasingly clear that the CCR was to remain a small minority within the church and that the church was more impervious to change than originally thought. In recent years the movement has experienced some of that loss of enthusiasm that appears to characterize the history of all such movements. While there are still many viable Catholic Charismatic communities and prayer groups dotting the landscape, growth rates have slowed or declined and meetings at all levels are more subdued in tone.

In one sense, the CCR is a victim of wider societal trends which parallelled its development and whose origins were related to some of the events that made the CCR possible. The late 1970s and 1980s in the United States saw a resurgence of interest in more traditional value patterns in a number of social institutions. Conservatism became more fashionable in politics, law, education, as well as religion. Some churches, Roman Catholic included, began reemphasizing exactly those things that the CCR had been stressing: a greater emphasis on the Bible, greater concern for stable family patterns, and a reexamination of the value of traditional sexual norms. Thus, the basic message of the CCR does not seem as unique and unusual as it once did. There are now more avenues for expressions of traditional values than existed at the time the CCR flourished.

None of the above is meant to indicate that the demise of the CCR is imminent. The likelihood is that, like other social movements of this kind, it will continue to maintain itself at least through this generation. However, its most noteworthy impact on the institutional church may be behind it. Issues of *New Covenant* that extend up through April, 1983, indicate that even Steve Clark is asking that crucial question, "Has the charismatic renewal peaked?" (Clark, 1982; 1983).

Movement leaders who are addressing this issue of malaise are once again stressing the importance of the Gifts of the Spirit. Like all those enthusiastic movements which preceeded it, the CCR is faced with the difficulties in maintaining commitment which accompany large size and routinization. Although most social organizations welcome increases in numbers, large size places irrepressible burdens on attempts to maintain a sense of community. Size tends to freeze status structures, to narrow and formalize communication channels, and to result in the increased alienation of members. Similarly, the routinization of even the most stimulating behavior eventually moderates its emotional impact. Without that emotional component, attraction and commitment wane.

In spite of the possible decreasing influence of the CCR, the questions it posed for the institutional church are still relevant. What issues, events, or elements of ritual can be counted on to promote unity and commitment within the church itself? The secularization trend that appeared to be accelerated by unanticipated outcomes of Post Vatican II experimentation shows little sign of abating. The ethnic church is no longer viable and able to provide a sense of community. That generation which somewhat automatically accepted church teaching and still remembers Wednesday night Rosary devotions and Novenas is fading from the scene. The institutional church has no effective counterpart to the CCR's commitment mechanisms nor does it appear likely that tongue speaking and prophecy are to become accepted practices among the bulk of practicing Roman Catholics.

It is clear that in this modern era churches which provide a sense of community and an opportunity for intense emotional involvement are much more successful in attracting members than those that do not (Zablocki, 1978). In that sense the CCR can be viewed as a messenger to a beleaguered church. It highlighted problems facing the institutional church and offered some means with which to address these problems. However, like the church, the CCR itself is becoming institutionalized and, like the church, is now searching for ways to continue to attract and commit members. It is likely that the CCR, like the many movements which tried to revitalize the church throughout history, will fade in significance. Its most committed members may eventually form another religious order which will take its place with those that are now part of the very fabric of the church such as the Franciscans. These kinds of movements have provided correctives to problems facing the church at various periods and have done much to preserve that organization as perhaps the oldest of all social organizations.

Bibliography

Abbott, W.M., S.J. (ed.). 1966. *The Documents of Vatican II.* London-Dublin: Geoffrey Chapman.

Aberle, D. 1965. A Note on Relative Deprivation Theory as Applied to Millenarian and Other Cult Movements. In W. Lessa and E. Vogt (eds.) *Reader in Comparative Religion.* New York: Harper and Row, pp. 527–531.

Allport, G.W., and J.M. Ross. 1967. Personal Religious Orientation and Prejudice. *Journal of Personality and Social Psychology* 5:432–443.

Aronson, E. 1972. *The Social Animal.* San Francisco: W.H. Freeman.

Asch, S.E. 1951. Effects of Group Pressure upon the Modification and Distortion of Judgments. In H. Guetzkow (ed.) *Groups, Leadership, and Men.* Pittsburgh: Carnegie Press, pp. 177–190.

Back, K.W. 1972. *Beyond Words.* New York: Russell Sage Foundation.

Bandura, A. 1977. Self-Efficacy: Toward a Unifying Theory of Behavioral Change. *Psychological Review* 84:191–215.

Basham, D. 1977. Why Do We Need the Spiritual Gifts. *New Covenant* 7:18–21.

Baum, G., L.S.A. 1969. Suenens Crying in the Wilderness. *The Catholic World* 10:103–107.

Becker, H. 1932. *Systematic Sociology.* New York: John Wiley.

Bell, D. 1971. Religion in the Sixties. *Social Research* Autumn:447–497.

Benson, J.K., and J.H. Dorsett. 1971. Toward a Typology of Religious Organizations. *Journal for the Scientific Study of Religion* 10:138–151.

Berger, P.L. 1967. *The Sacred Canopy.* Garden City, N.Y. Doubleday.

Blattner, J. 1979. On the Threshold. *New Covenant* 8:10–15.

Bonnell, J.S. 1968. *Do You Want to Be Healed?* New York: Harper and Row.

Bord, R.J., and J.E. Faulkner. 1975. Religiosity and Secular Attitudes: The Case of Catholic Pentecostals. *Journal for the Scientific Study of Religion* 14:257–270.

Bourguignon, E. (Ed.) 1973. *Religion, Altered States of Consciousness, and Social Change.* Columbus, Ohio: Ohio State University Press.

Brehm, J.W. 1966. *A Theory of Psychological Reactance*. New York: Academic Press.

Bromley, D.G., and A.D. Shupe, Jr. 1980. Financing the New Religions: A Resource Mobilization Perspective. *Journal for the Scientific Study of Religion* 19:227–39.

———. 1979. *"Moonies" in America: Cult, Church and Crusade*. Beverly Hills, CA: SAGE Publications.

Buck, R.C. 1979. Power of "the Word" in Tourism Promotion: Outlook for the Importance of Nostalgia and Romanticism in Tourism Development and Marketing. Paper delivered at Tourism and the Next Decade, an International Symposium. March 11–15, The George Washington University, Washington, D.C.

Cantril, H. 1941. *The Social Psychology of Social Movements* New York: John Wiley.

Cavnar, J. 1974. Spiritual Gifts at Prayer Meetings. *New Covenant* 2:25–27.

———. 1975. Spiritual Gifts in the Prayer Meeting. *New Covenant* 5:12–15.

Chapple, E. 1970. *Culture and Biological Man*. New York: Holt.

Cirner, R. 1974. Deliverence. *New Covenant* 3:4–7.

Clark, E.T. 1949. *The Small Sects in America*, revised edition. New York: Abington-Cokesbury.

Clark, S.B. 1965. *Freedom in the Cursillo*. Lansing, Mich.: National Cursillo Secretariat Publications.

———. 1972a. *Building Christian Communities: Strategy for Renewing the Church*. Notre Dame, Ind.: Ave Maria Press.

———. 1972b. Social Action: Strategy and Priorities. *New Covenant* 5:8–9.

———. 1973. *The Life in the Spirit Seminars: Team Manual*, 3rd edition. Ann Arbor, Mich.: Charismatic Renewal Services, Inc.

———. 1975. *Unordained Elders and Renewal Communities*. New York: Paulist Press.

———. 1982. "Renewing the Renewal." *New Covenant* 12:20–21.

———. 1983. "Are we charismatic?" *New Covenant* 12:24–25.

Clark, S.D. 1948. *Church and Sect in Canada*. Toronto: University of Toronto Press.

Cohn, W. 1968. Personality, Pentecostalism, and Glossolalia: A Research Note on Some Unsuccessful Research. *Canadian Review of Sociology and Anthropology* February:36–39.

Colaianni, J. 1968. *The Catholic Left: The Crisis of Radicalism in the Church*. New York: Chilton Book Company.

Coutourier, A. 1964. Mortification for the Sake of Others, Cursillo Style. *Ave Maria* 99:10–13.

Cox, H. 1965. *The Secular City*. New York: Macmillan.

———. 1971. *The Feast of Fools*. Cambridge, Mass.: Harvard University Press.

Demerath, N.J. 1967. In a Sow's Ear: A Reply to Goode. *Journal for the Scientific Study of Religion* 6:77–84.

Demerath, N.J., and P.E. Hammond. 1969. *Religion in Social Context*. New York: Random House.

Dittes, J. E. 1969. Psychology of Religion. In G. Lindzey and E. Aronson (eds.) *The Handbook of Social Psychology*, 2nd edition, Volume 5. Reading, Mass.: Addison-Wesley Publishing Company, pp. 602–659.

Dozier, Bishop C.T. 1973. Choose Life. *New Covenant* 3:25–26.

Dulles, A. 1974. *Models of the Church*. New York: Doubleday.

duPlessis, D. 1974. Persecution for Charismatic Catholics? *New Covenant* 3:13.

Durkheim, E. 1912. *The Elementary Forms of the Religious Life*. Trans. J. W. Swain. Glencoe, Ill. Free Press.

———. 1951 *Suicide*. Trans. George Simpson. New York: Free Press.

Duvan, Rev. A.M. 1962. *The Cursillo in Christianity Movement*. Phoenix, Ariz. Ultreya Press.

Elinson, H. 1965. The Implications of Pentecostal Religion for Intellectualism, Politics, and Race Relations. *American Journal of Sociology* 70:403–415.

Etzioni, A. 1961. *A Comparative Analysis of Complex Organizations*. New York: Free Press.

Fesquet, H. 1970. Cardinal Suenens: A Plea for Dialogue. *The Catholic World* 211:216–220.

Festinger, L. 1957. *A Theory of Cognitive Dissonance*. Stanford, Calif.: Stanford University Press.

Festinger, L., S. Schachter, and H. Reicken. 1956. *When Prophecy Fails*. Minneapolis: University of Minnesota Press.

Fichter, J.H. 1975. *The Catholic Cult of the Paraclete*. New York: Sheed and Ward.

Ford, J.M. 1970. *The Pentecostal Experience*. New York: Paulist Press.

Forrest, Fr. T. 1974. Tongues: A Gift of Roses. *New Covenant* 4:30–32.

Frank, J. 1973. *Persuasion and Healing*. Baltimore: Johns Hopkins Press.

Franks, D.D., and J. Marolla. 1976. Efficacious Action and Social Approval as Interacting Dimensions of Self Esteem: A Tentative Formulation Through Construct Validation. *Sociometry*. 39:324–340.

French, J.R.P., and B.H. Raven. 1959. The Basis of Social Power. In D. Cartwright (ed.) *Studies in Social Power*. Ann Arbor: University of Michigan Press.

Gamson, W.A. 1975. *The Strategy of Social Protest*. Homewood, Ill.: Dorsey Press.

Gardner, H. 1978. *The Children of Prosperity*. New York: St. Martin's Press.

Gavrilides, G. 1976. Sexual Control: Is It Possible? *New Covenant* 5:8–10.

Gelpi, D.L. 1971. *Pentecostalism: A Theological Viewpoint*. New York: Paulist Press.

Gerlach, L.P. 1974. Pentecostalism: Revolution or Counter-Revolution? In I. I. Zaretsky and M. P. Leone (eds.) *Religious Movements in Contemporary America*. Princeton, N.J.: Princeton University Press, pp. 669–699.

Gerlach, L.P., and V.H. Hine. 1970. *People, Power, Change: Movements of Social Transformation*. New York: Bobbs-Merrill.

Gerth, H.H., and C.W. Mills. 1946. *Max Weber: Essays in Sociology*. New York: Oxford University Press.

Ghezzi, B. 1975. A Joyful Pilgrimage: Report on the 1975 International Conference. *New Covenant* 5:14–22.

Gilmore, S.K. 1969. Personality Differences Between High and Low Dogmatism Groups of Pentecostal Believers. *Journal for the Scientific Study of Religion* 8:161–164.

Glass, D.C., and J.E. Singer. 1972. *Urban Stress: Experiments on Noise and Social Stressors.* New York: Academic Press.

Goffman, E. 1959. *The Presentation of Self in Everyday Life.* Garden City, N.Y.: Doubleday.

Goodman, F.D. 1972. *Speaking in Tongues.* Chicago: University of Chicago Press.

Greeley, A. 1972. *The Denominational Society.* Glenview, Ill.: Scott, Foresman.

Harrison, M.I. 1974. Sources of Recruitment to Catholic Pentecostalism. *Journal for the Scientific Study of Religion* 13:49–64.

Hine, V. 1969. Pentecostal Glossolalia: Toward a Functional Interpretation. *Journal for the Scientific Study of Religion* 8:211–226.

———. 1974. The Deprivation and Disorganization Theories of Social Movements. In I. I. Zaretsky and M. P. Leone (eds.) *Religious Movements in Contemporary America.* Princeton, N.J.: Princeton University Press, pp. 646–661.

Hollenweger, W.J. 1972. *The Pentecostals.* Minneapolis, Minn.: Augsburg.

Hunter, E. 1951. *Brainwashing in Red China.* New York: Vanguard Press.

Jahr, M.A. 1974. A Turning Point. *New Covenant* 21:4–7.

Keene, J. 1967. Religious Behavior and Neuroticism, Spontaneity, and World-mindedness. *Sociometry* 30:137–157.

Kelsey, M.T. 1973. *Healing and Christianity.* New York: Harper and Row.

Kildahl, J.P. 1972. *The Psychology of Speaking in Tongues.* New York: Harper and Row.

Knox, R.A. 1950. *Enthusiasm: A Chapter in the History of Religion.* New York: Oxford University Press.

Lange, J. 1976. Editorial. *Catholic Charismatic* 1:2.

Levi, Ken (ed.). 1982. *Violence and Religious Commitment: Implications of Jim Jones's People's Temple Movement.* University Park, Pa.: Penn State Press.

Lifton, R.J. 1961. *Thought Reform and the Psychology of Totalism.* New York: W.W. Norton.

Lovekin, A., and H.N. Maloney. 1977. Religious Glossolalia: A Longitudinal Study of Personality Changes. *Journal for the Scientific Study of Religion* 16:383–393.

McCarthy, J., and M. Zald. 1977. Resource Mobilization and Social Movements: A Partial Theory. *American Journal of Sociology* 82:1212–1241.

McCormick, R.A., S.J. 1964. Whither the Pill. *The Catholic World* 199:207–215.

McDonnell, K. 1976. A Churchless Christianity. *New Covenant* 5:26–29.

———. 1977. Protestants, Pentecostals, and Mary. *New Covenant* 6:26–29.

———. 1978. Prayer Groups and Communities. *New Covenant* 8:23–27.

McKinney, Bishop J. 1973. An Open Letter to Catholic Charismatics. *New Covenant* 3:10–11.

MacNutt, Fr. F. 1974. *Healing.* Notre Dame, Ind. Ave Maria Press.

———. 1975. Should a Christian Expect Healing? *New Covenant* 4:12–14.

Mahoney, M.J. 1974. *Cognition and Behavior Modification.* Cambridge, Mass.: Ballinger.

Manney, Jim. 1973. Before Duquesne: Sources of the Renewal. *New Covenant* 2:12–17.

Martin, G. 1976. How Can You Help Your Parish? *New Covenant* 5:8–12.

Martin, R. 1971. *Unless the Lord Build the House*. Notre Dame, Ind.: Ave Maria Press.

———. 1974. Confronting the Reality of Satan. *New Covenant* 3:3.

———. 1974. David Wilkerson's Vision. *New Covenant* 3:11–12.

———. 1974. God Is Restoring His People. *New Covenant* 4:3–6.

———. 1978. Perspective: Parish Renewal or Covenant Community? *New Covenant*. 8:20–22.

Marty, M. 1968. A Warning to Catholic Extremists. *America* 119:122–125.

Marx, K. 1936. *Capital*. New York: Modern Library.

Maslow, A.H. 1970. *Religions, Values, and Peak Experiences*. New York: Viking Press.

Moscovici, S., and C. Faucheaux. 1972. Social Influence, Conformity Bias, and the Study of Active Minorities. In L. Berkowitz (ed.) *Advances in Experimental Social Psychology*, Volume 6. New York: Academic Press.

National Catholic Reporter. August 1975a. Charismatics Pledge Spiritual Warfare. 11:1.

———. August 1975b. In Bar or Car, Praise the Lord. 11:3,16.

———. September 1975. The Charismatics. 11:3.

Nee, W. 1965. *The Release of the Spirit*. Cloverdale, Ind.: Ministry of Life.

New Covenant. October 1973. God's Word to Us. 3:23.

———. December 1973. International Leaders Meet with Pope Paul. 3:5.

———. January 1974a. A Statement of the Theological Basis of the Catholic Charismatic Renewal. 3:21–23.

———. January 1974b. Service Committee Issues Ecumenical Statement. 3:19–20.

———. April 1974. Satan and Catholic Tradition. 3:8–9.

———. July 1974. An interview with Fr. Heribert Muhlen: Theologian of the Holy Spirit. 4:3–6.

———. September 1974. A Prophetic Vision. 4:7–9.

———. March 1975. A God of Power: Healing Testimonies from the 1974 International Conference of the Catholic Charismatic Renewal. 4:18–20.

———. July 1975a. Pope Paul Addresses the Charismatic Renewal. 5:23–25.

———. July 1975b. Prophecies given at St. Peter's Basilica During the Closing Eucharist on Pentecost Monday. 5:26.

———. November 1975. A Statement Concerning a Recent Controversy. 5:22–23.

———. December 1975. Authority in Christian Communities: Interview with Steve Clark. 5:24–27.

———. April 1976. Healing: Some Problems and Issues. 5:15–18.

———. November 1976. The Parish and the Charismatic Renewal: An Interview with John Randall. 6:21–23.

———. January 1978. The State of the Catholic Church. 7:4–8.

———. February 1978. How Should We Respond? An Interview with Kevin Ranaghan. 7:10–13.

New York Times. September 8, 1974. Charismatic Renewal is Flourishing in the Churches.

Nichol, J.T. 1966. *Pentecostalism*. New York: Harper and Row.

Niebuhr, H.R. 1929. *The Social Sources of Denominationalism.* New York: Henry Holt.

Nolen, W.A., M.D. 1974. *Healing: A Doctor in Search of a Miracle.* New York: Random House.

Oberschall, A. 1973. *Social Conflict and Social Movements.* Englewood Cliffs, N.J.: Prentice-Hall.

O'Connor, Fr. E.D., C.S.C. 1971. *The Pentecostal Movement in the Catholic Church.* Notre Dame, Ind.: Ave Maria Press.

———. 1975. Discernment of Spirits: Part I. *New Covenant.* 4:10–13; Part II. *New Covenant* 4:31–33; Part III. *New Covenant.* 4:26–29.

Parsons, T. 1951. *The Social System.* New York: Free Press.

Pattison, E.M., and R.L. Carey. 1969. Glossolalia: A Contemporary Mystical Experience. In E.M. Pattison (ed.) *Clinical Psychiatry and Religion* 5:133–148.

Perrow, C. 1979. The Sixties Observed. In M.N. Zald and J.D. McCarthy (eds.) *The Dynamics of Social Movements.* Cambridge, Mass.: Winthrop Publishers.

Pope, L. 1942. *Millhands and Preachers.* New Haven: Yale University Press.

Ranaghan, K. 1972. Our Future Is Charismatic. *New Catholic World* 215:261–263.

Ranaghan, K. and D. Ranaghan. 1969 *Catholic Pentecostals.* Paramus, N.J.: Paulist Press.

———. 1971. *As the Spirit Leads Us.* Paramus, N. J.: Paulist Press.

Samarian, W.J. 1972. *Tongues of Men and Angels.* New York: Macmillan.

Schein, E.H. 1961. *Coercive Persuasion.* New York: Norton.

Schiffer, I., M.D. 1973. *Charisma.* Toronto: University of Toronto Press.

Scott, J.F. 1971. *Internalization of Norms: A Sociological Theory of Moral Commitment.* Englewood Cliffs, N.J.: Prentice-Hall.

Seligman, M.E.P. 1975. *Helplessness: On Depression, Development, and Death.* San Francisco: W.H. Freeman.

Selznick, P. 1943. An Approach to the Theory of Bureaucracy. *American Sociological Review* 8:47–54.

Shaw, M.E., and P.R. Costanzo. 1970. *Theories of Social Psychology.* New York: McGraw-Hill.

Sheehan, Dr. G. 1975. *Dr. Sheehan on Running.* Mountain View, Calif.: World Publications.

Sheerin, J.B., C.S.P. 1970. Civil War in the Church. *The Catholic World* 210:194–195.

Sherrill, J.L. 1965. *They Speak with Other Tongues.* Spire Books, N.J.: Fleming H. Revell Co. First Published in 1964.

Sills, D. 1970. Preserving Organizational Goals. In O. Grusky and G. A. Miller (eds.) *The Sociology of Organizations.* New York: Free Press, pp. 227–236.

Skinner, B.F. 1953. *Science and Human Behavior.* New York: Macmillan.

Smelser, N.J. 1963. *Theory of Collective Behavior.* New York: Free Press Glencoe. Orginally published in 1962.

Suenens, Cardinal L.J. 1975. *A New Pentecost:* New York: Seabury Press.

———. 1977. The First Decade of the Catholic Charismatic Renewal. *New Covenant* 6:13–14.

Synan, V. 1971. *The Holiness-Pentecostal Movement in the United States.* Grand Rapids, Mich.: William B. Eerdmans.

Tavard, G.H. 1967. *The Pilgrim Church.* New York: Herder and Herder.

Teilhard deChardin, P. 1959. *The Phenomenon of Man.* Trans. Bernard Wall. London: Wm. Collins.

Tilly, C. 1978 *From Mobilization to Revolution.* Reading, Mass.: Addison-Wesley.

Tonnies, F. 1963. *Gemeinschaft und Gesselschaft.* Translated and edited by C.P. Loomis as *Community and Society.* New York: Harper and Row.

Trepanier, J.R. 1968. The Cursillo Movement in the Light of Vatican Council II's Decree "On the Apostolate of the Laity." M.A. Thesis. Washington, D.C.: Catholic University of America.

Troeltsch. E. 1931. *The Social Teachings of the Christian Churches.* Trans. Olive Wyon. London: Allen and Unwin.

Turner, R., and L. Killian. 1972. *Collective Behavior.* Englewood Cliffs, N.J.: Prentice-Hall.

Van Buren, P. 1963. *The Secular Meaning of the Gospel.* New York: Macmillan.

Wallace, C. 1965. Pacem in Terris, Ecclesiam Suam and Communism. *Catholic World* 200:231–238.

Walsh, E.J. 1981. Resource Mobilization and Citizen Protest in Communities around Threee Mile Island. *Social Problems* 29:1–21.

Weber, M. 1930. *The Protestant Ethic and the Spirit of Capitalism.* London: Allen and Unwin.

White, R.W. 1959. Motivation Reconsidered: The Concept of Competence. *Psychological Review* 66:297–333.

Wilkerson, D. 1964. *The Cross and the Switchblade.* New York: Pyramid Books.

Willebrands, Cardinal J. 1975. The Holy Spirit and the Church. *New Covenant* 5:24–26.

Williams, J.R. 1978. Why Speak in Tongues? *New Covenant* 7:14–16.

Wills, G. 1965. Brainwashing . . . For God's Sake? *National Catholic Reporter* February 17.

Wilson, B.R. 1959. An Analysis of Sect Development. *American Sociological Review* 24:13–15.

Wood, W.W. 1965. *Culture and Personality Aspects of the Pentecostal Holiness Religion.* The Hague: Mouton.

Yinger, J.M. 1970. *The Scientific Study of Religion.* New York: Macmillan.

Zablocki, Benjamin D. 1978. Communes, encounter groups, and the search for community. In K.W. Back (ed.) *In Search for Community: Encounter Groups and Social Change.* Washington, D.C.: Westview Press. pp. 97–139.

Index